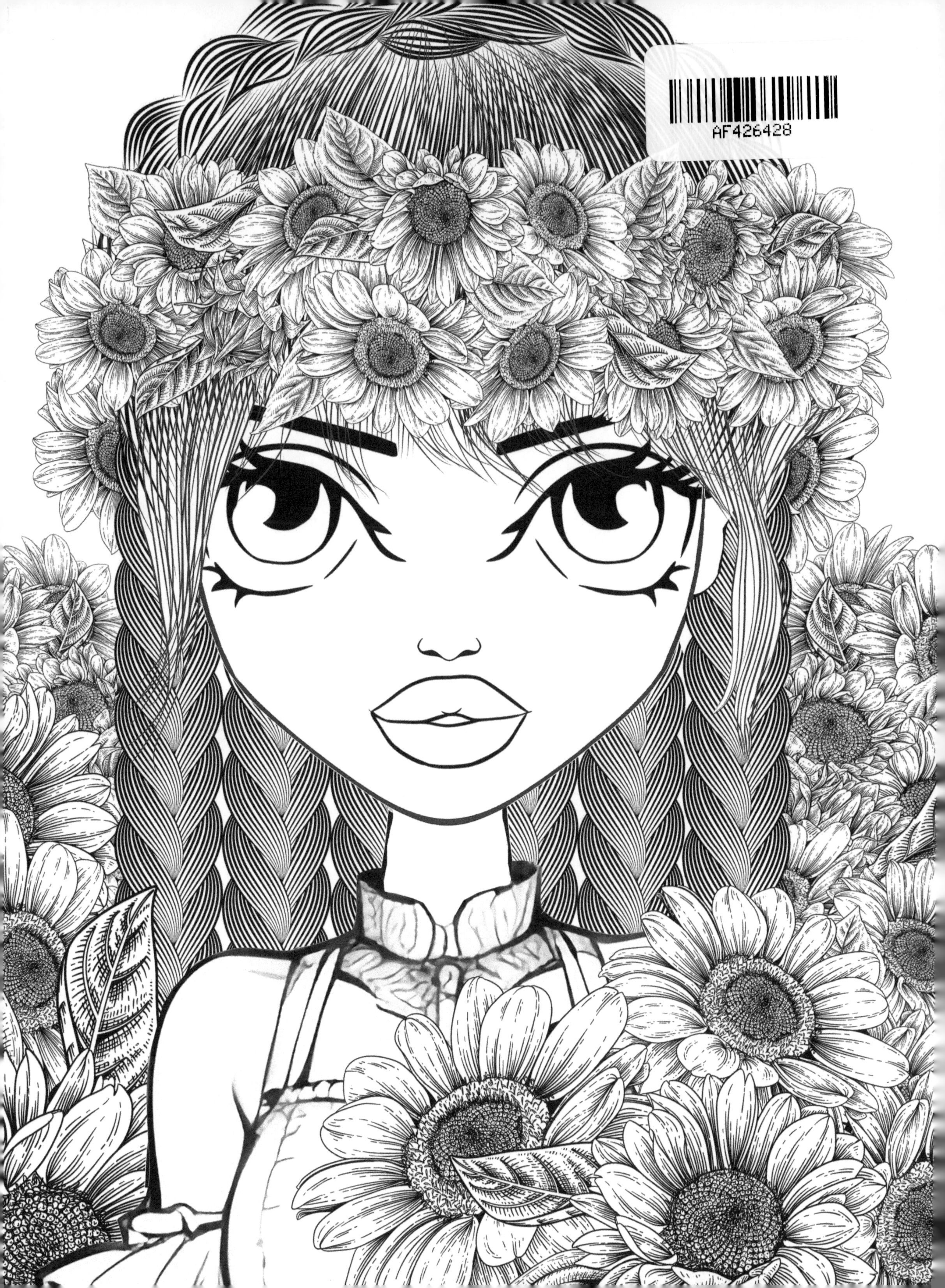
AF426428

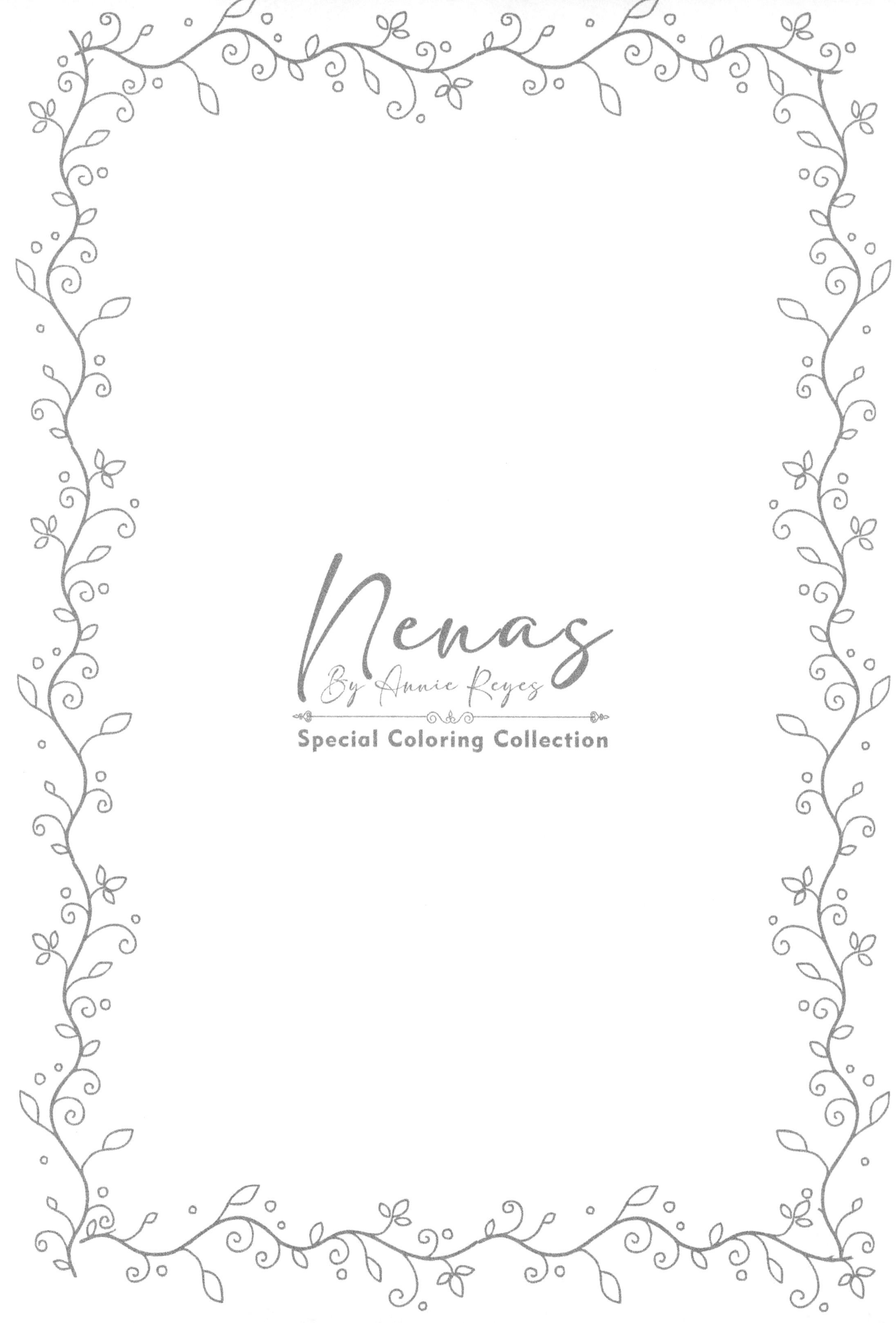

Nenas
By Annie Reyes
Special Coloring Collection

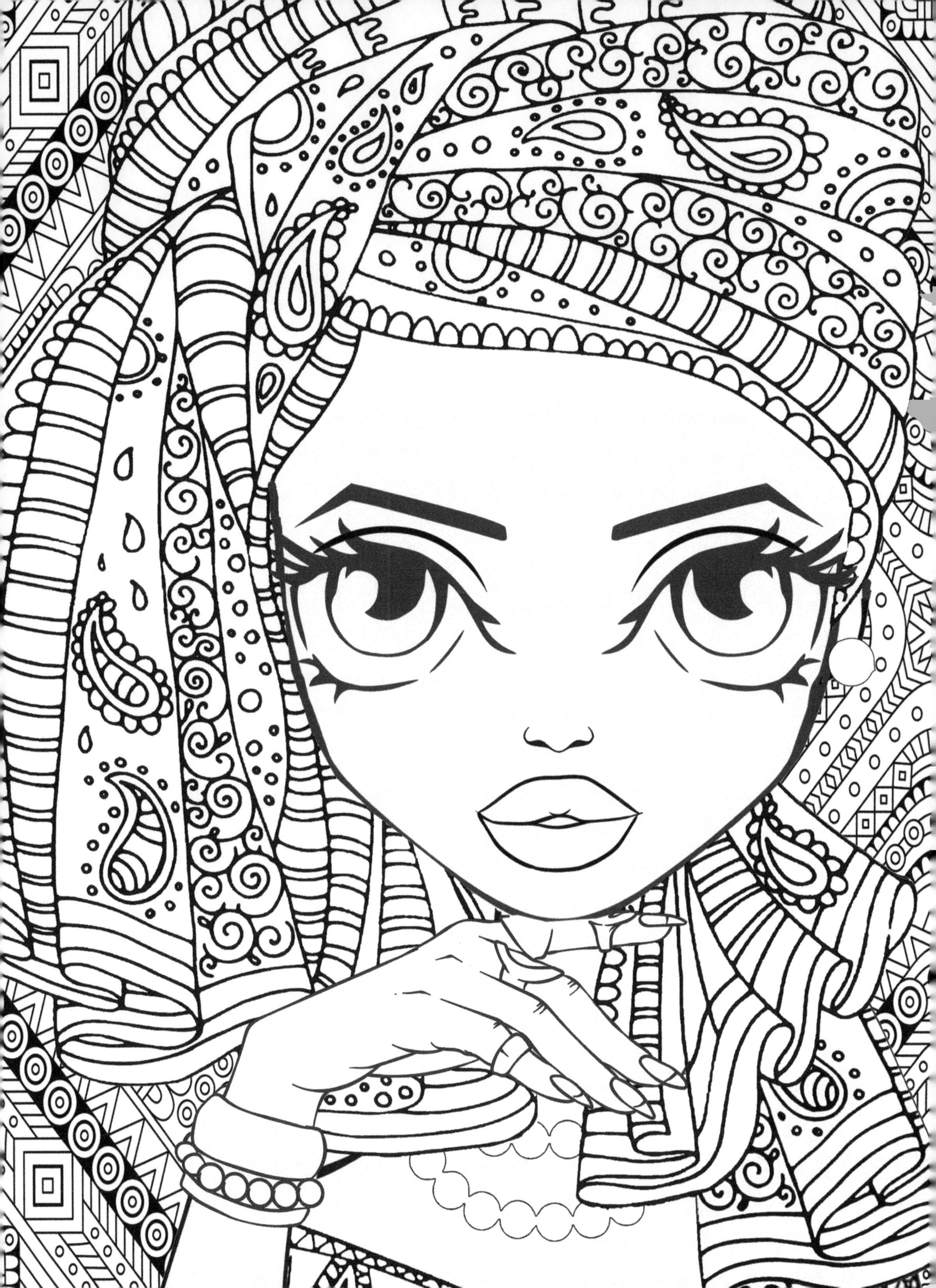

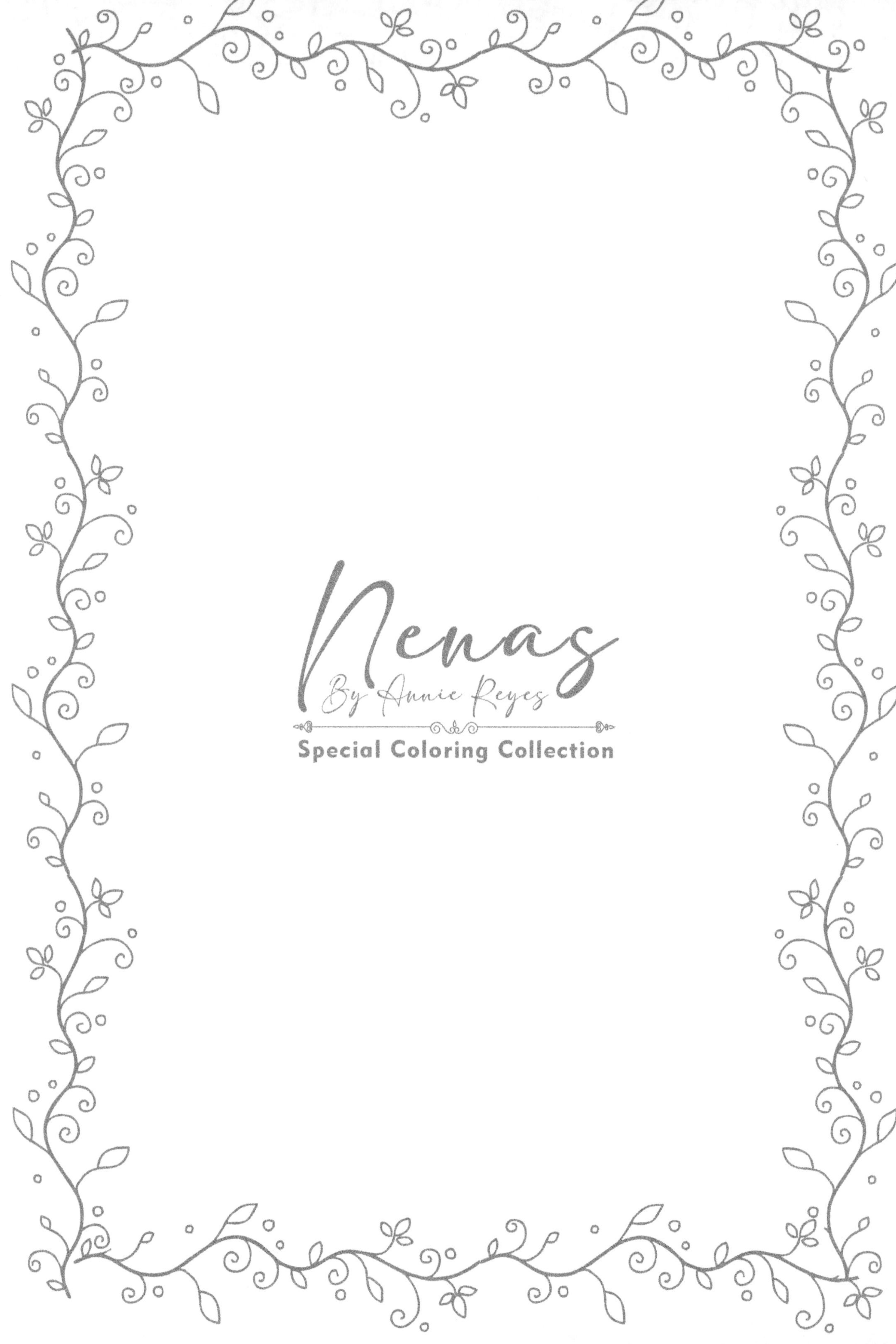

Nenas
By Annie Reyes
Special Coloring Collection

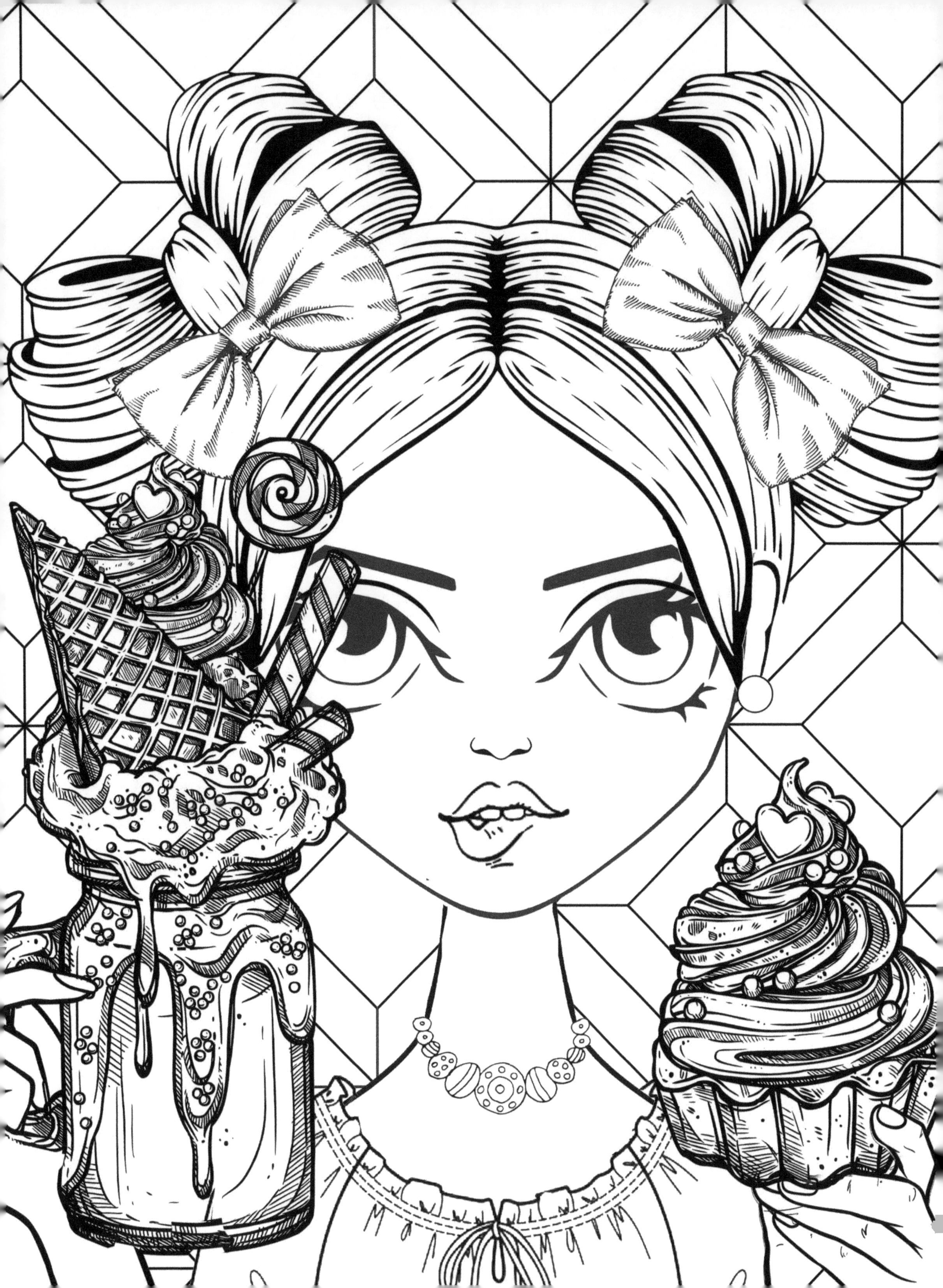

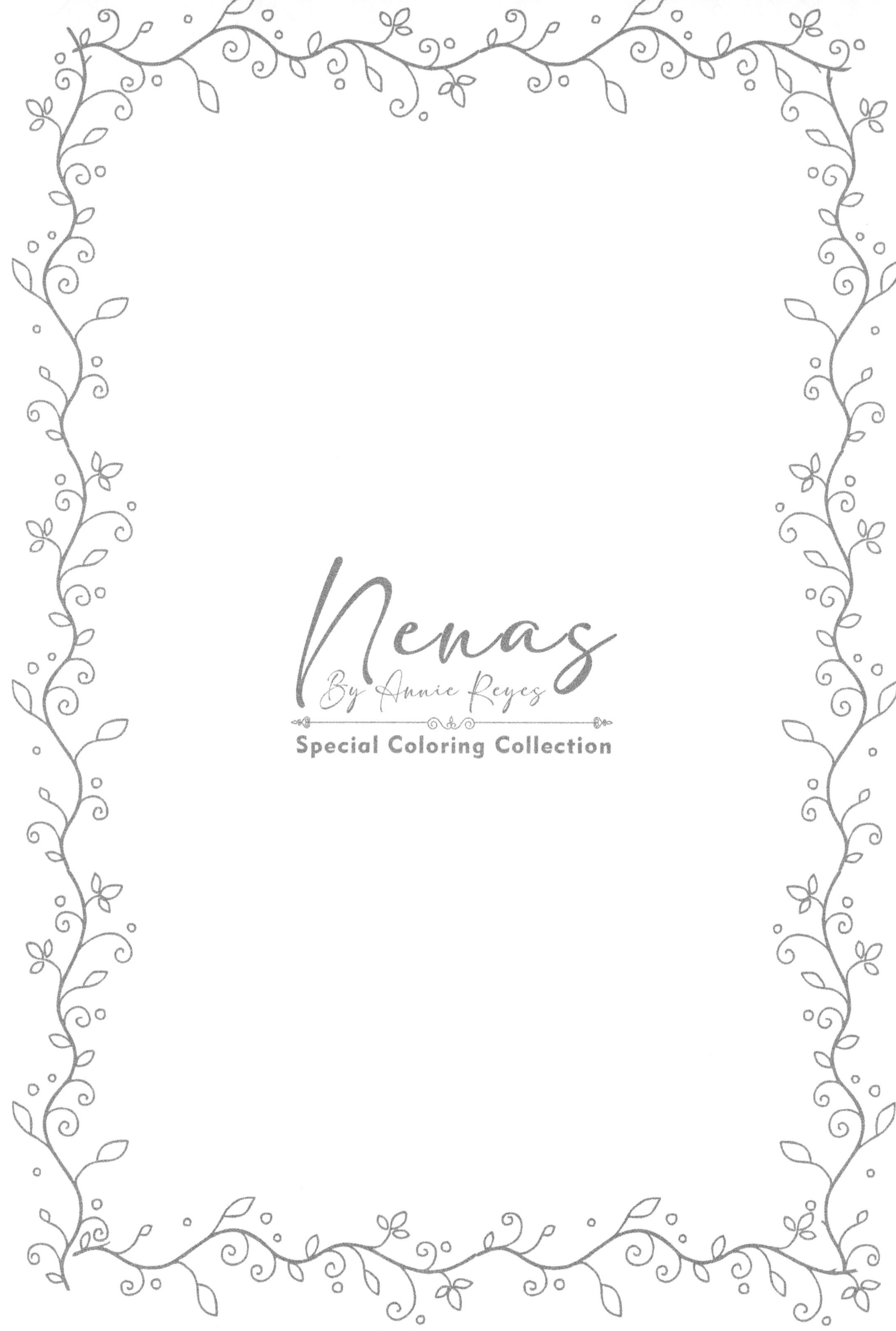

Nenas
By Annie Reyes
Special Coloring Collection

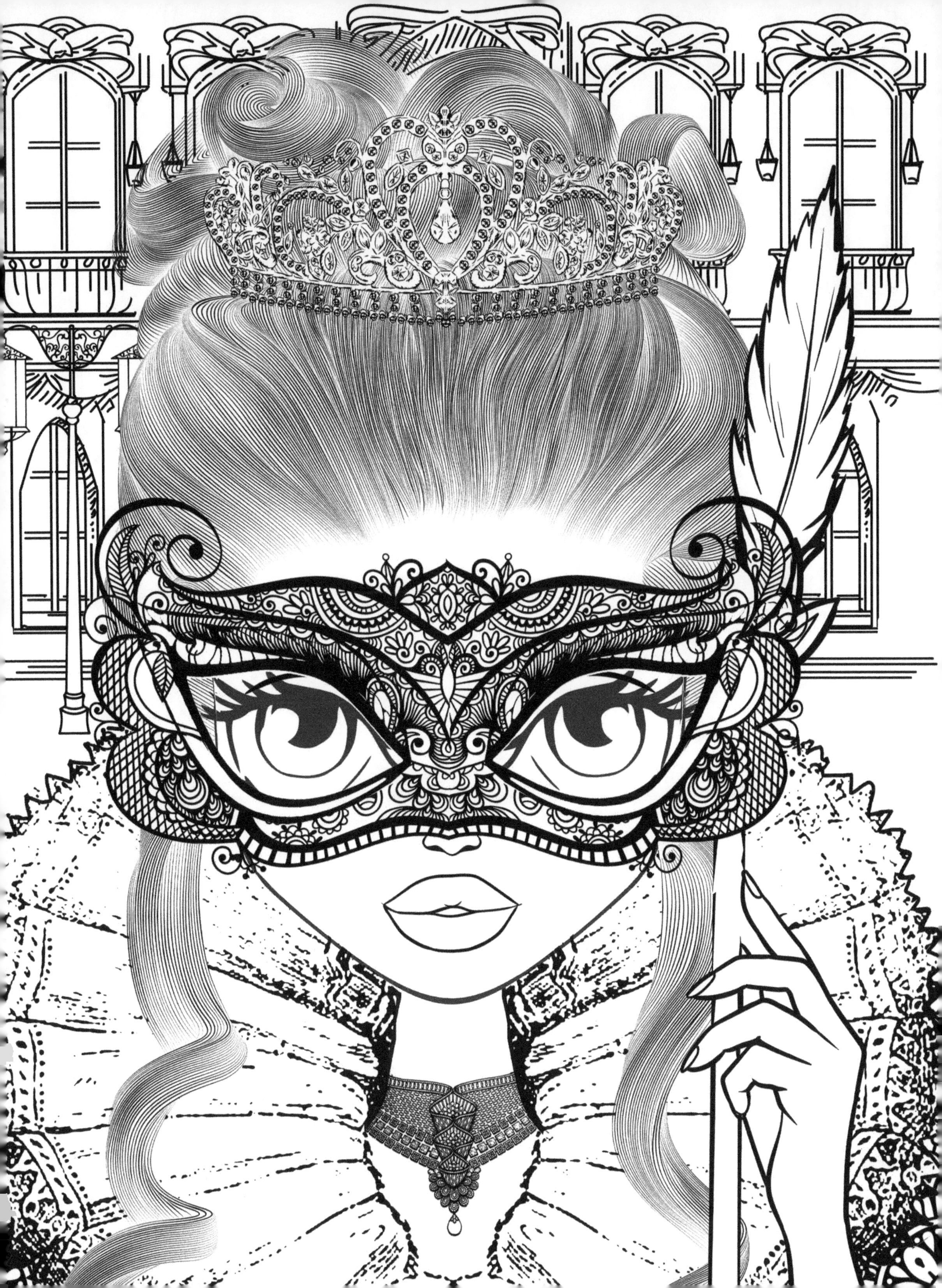

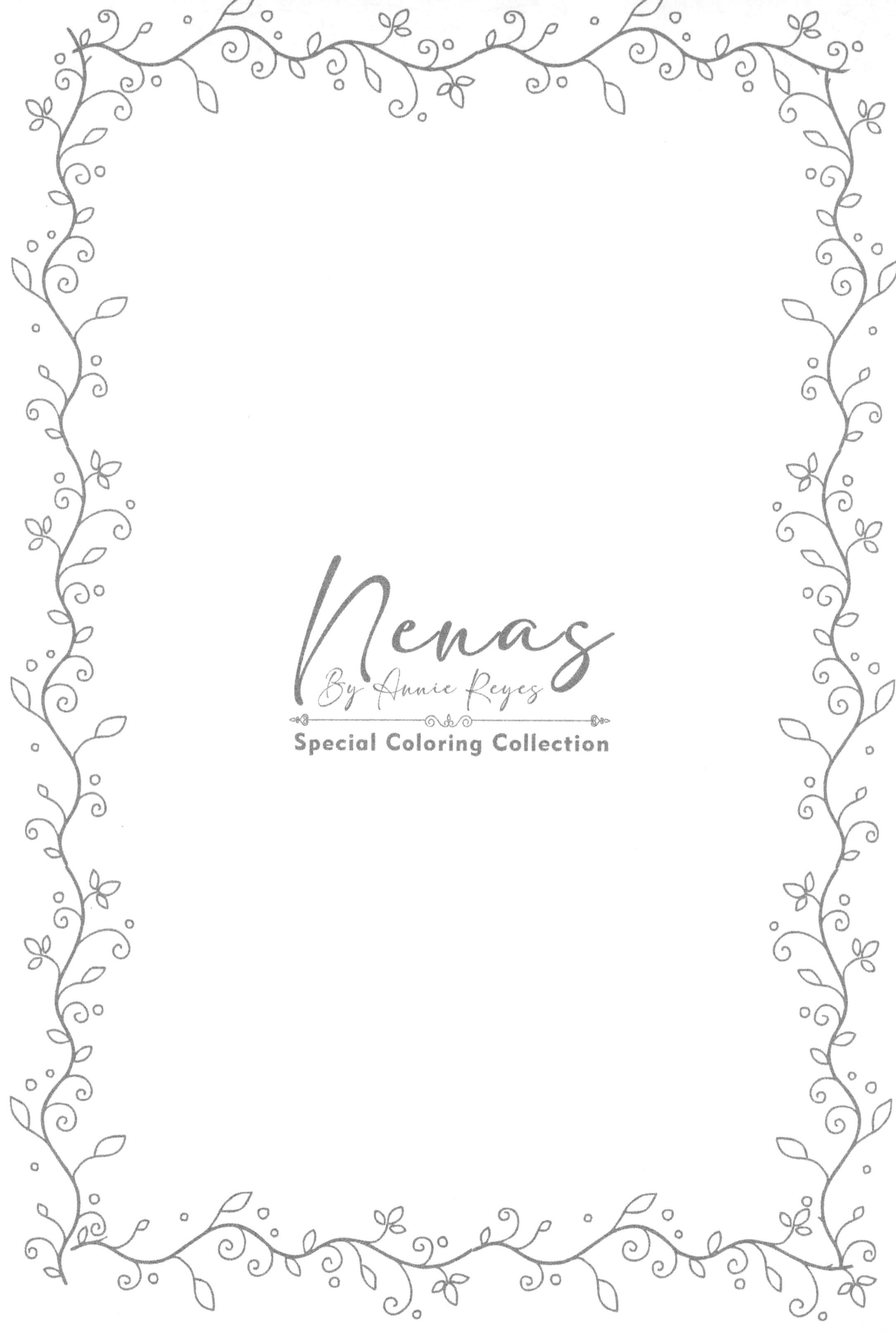

Nenas
By Annie Reyes
Special Coloring Collection

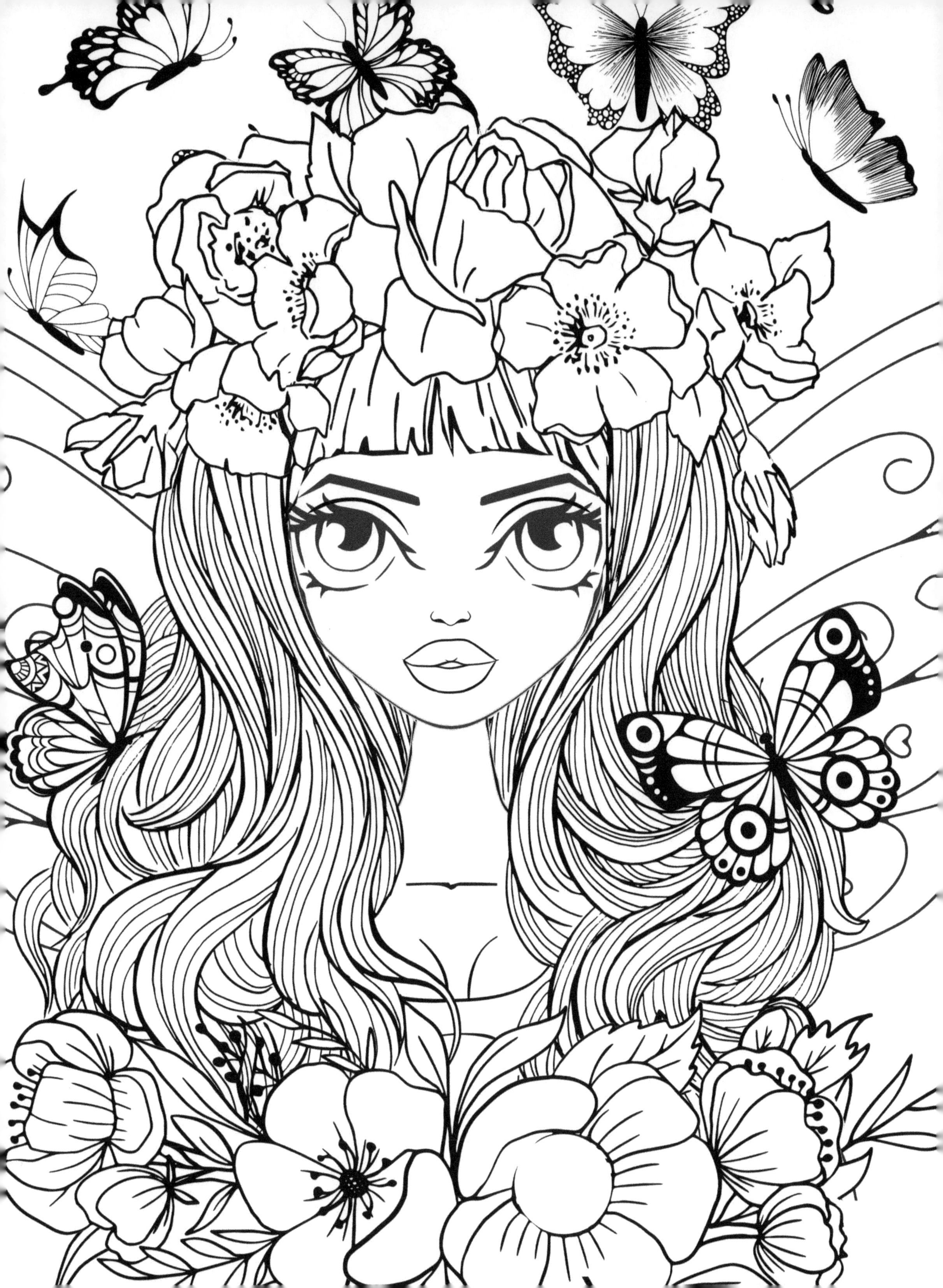

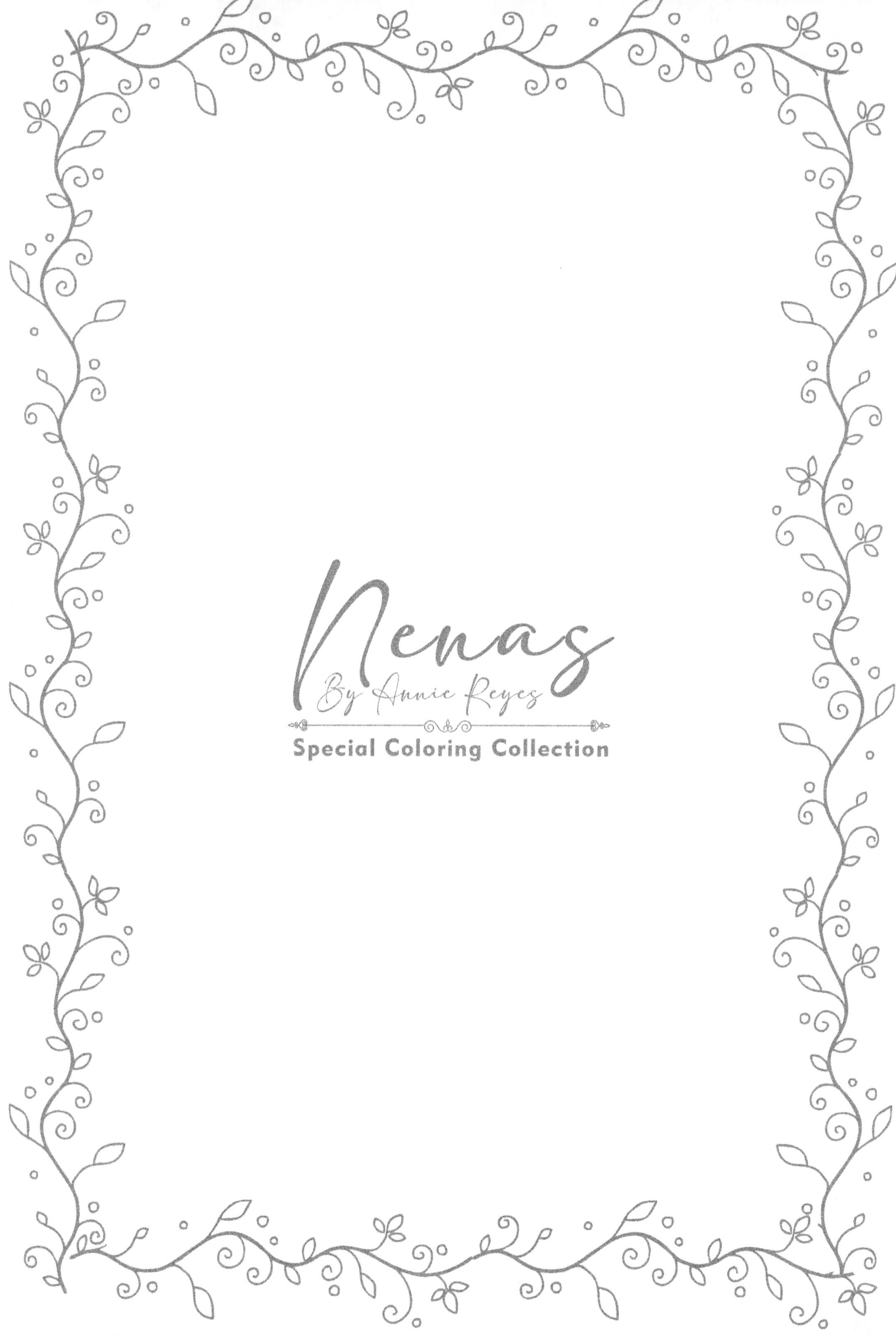

Nenas
By Annie Reyes
Special Coloring Collection

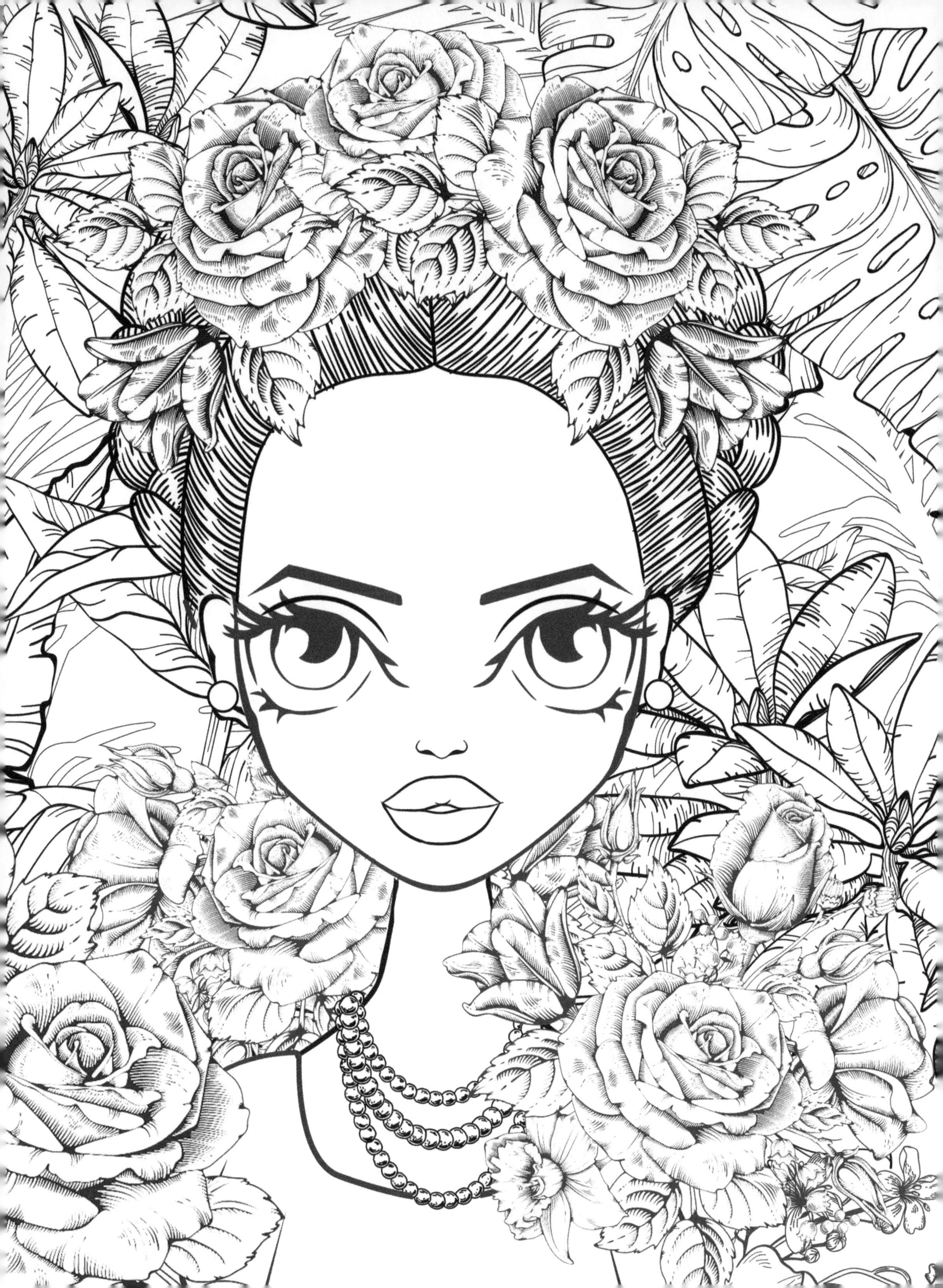

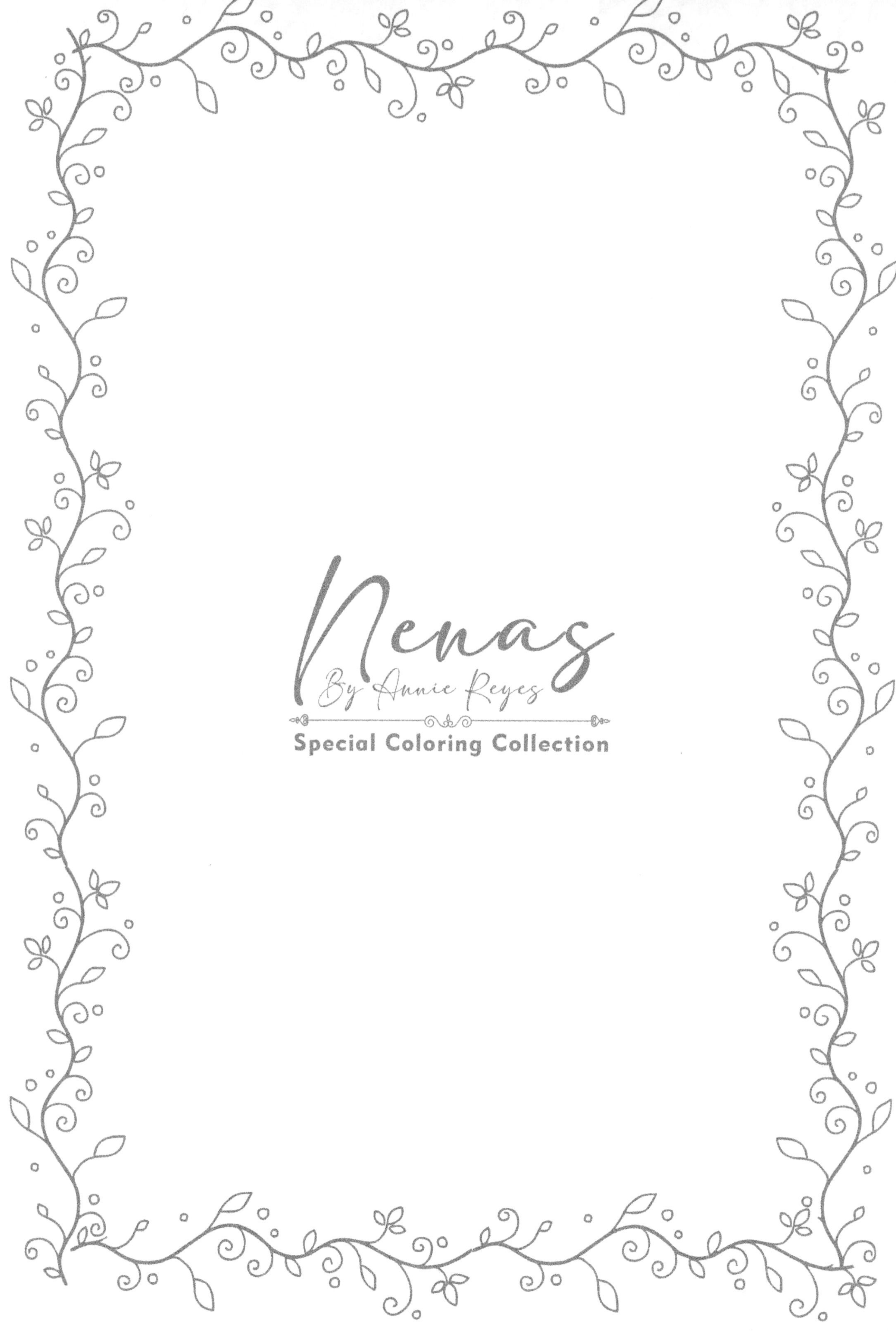

Nenas
By Annie Reyes
Special Coloring Collection

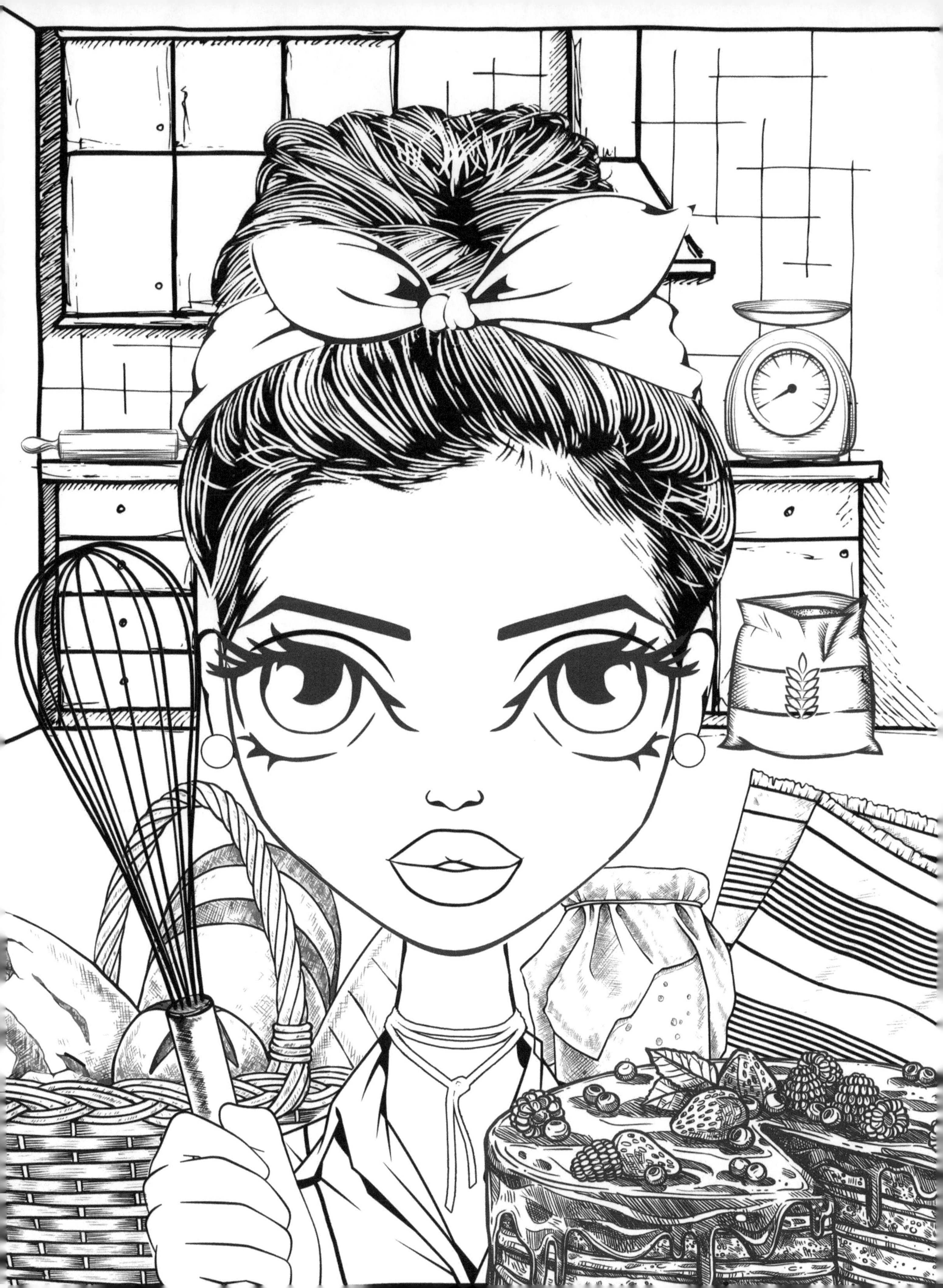

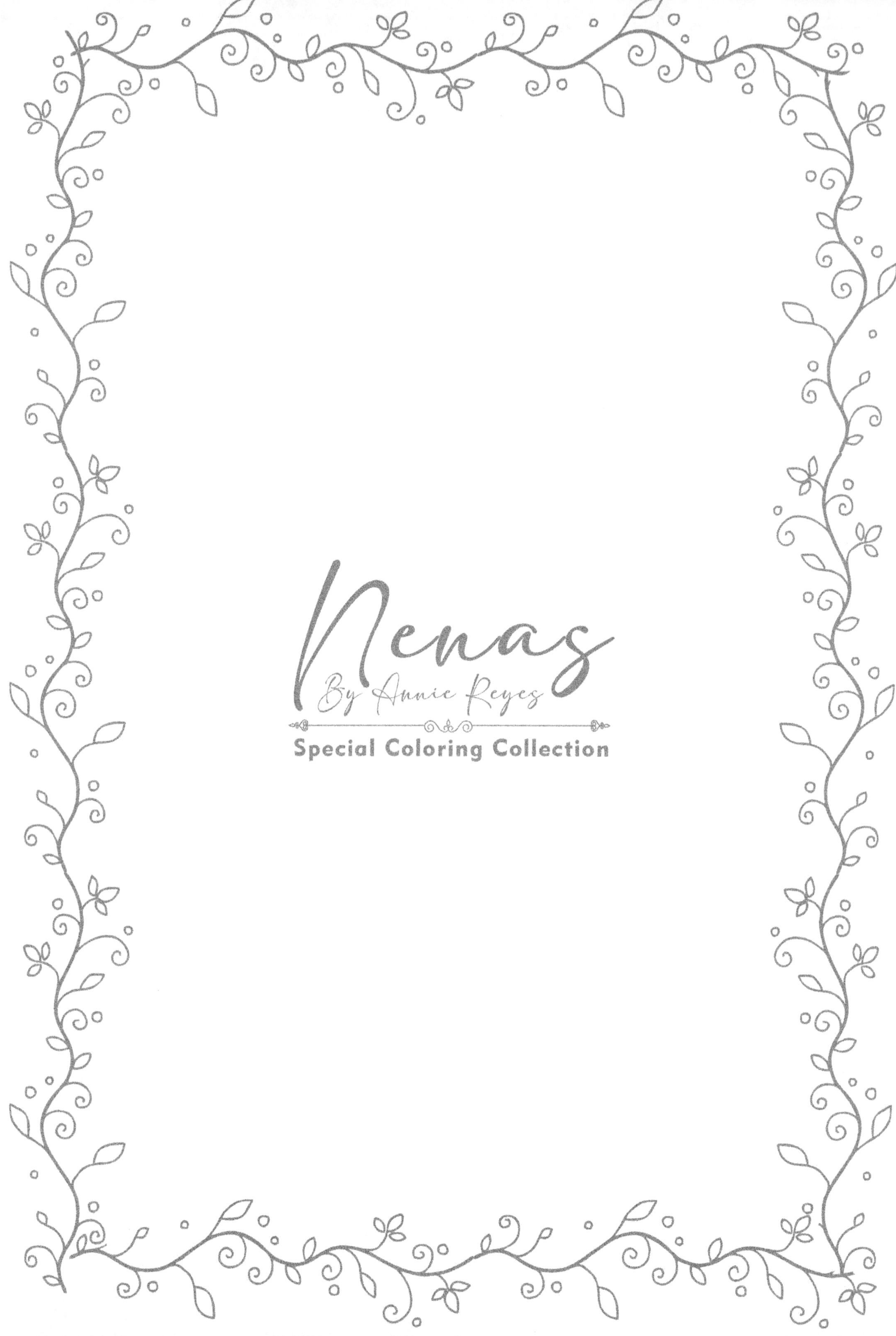

Nenas
By Annie Reyes
Special Coloring Collection

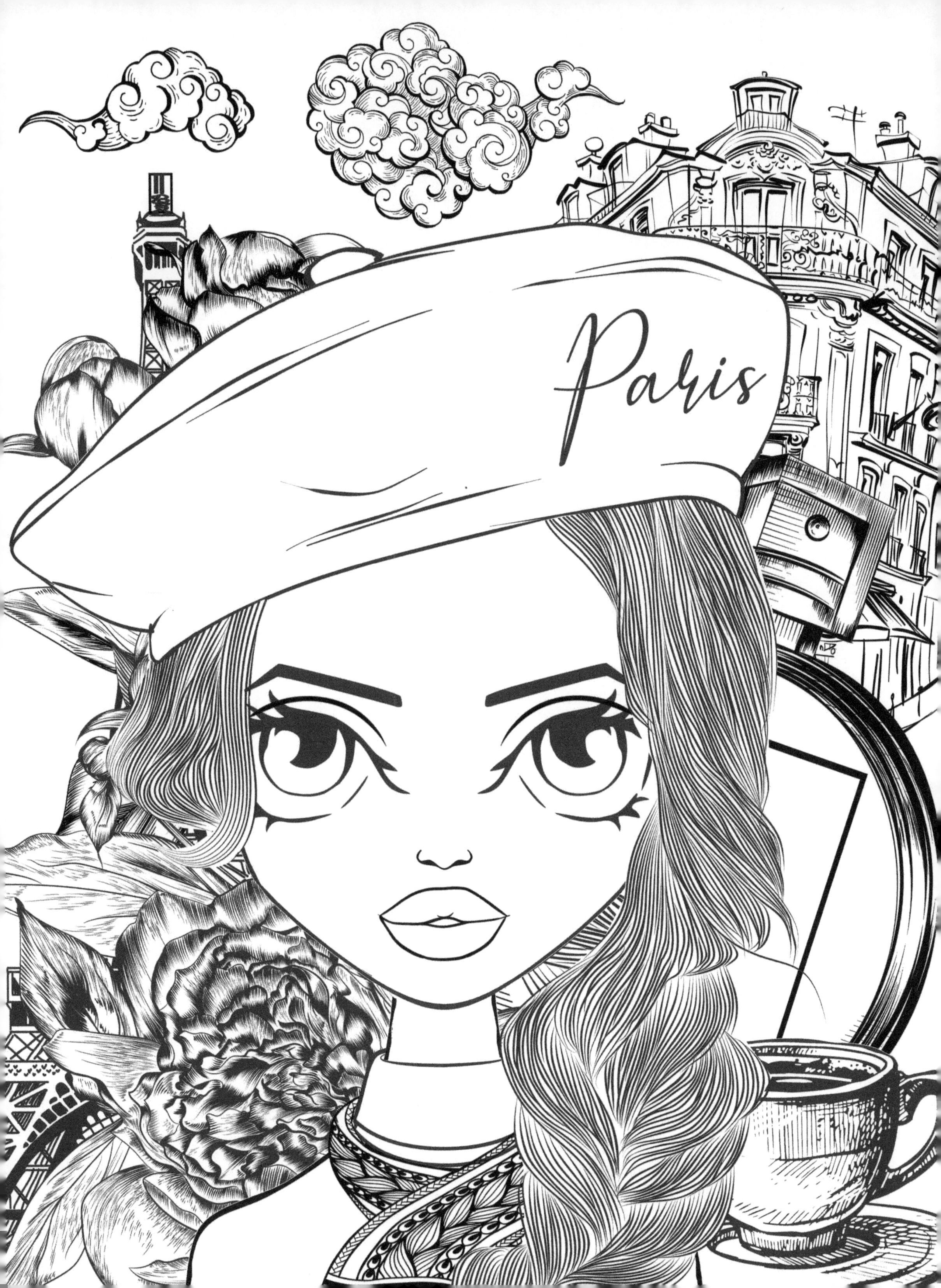
Paris

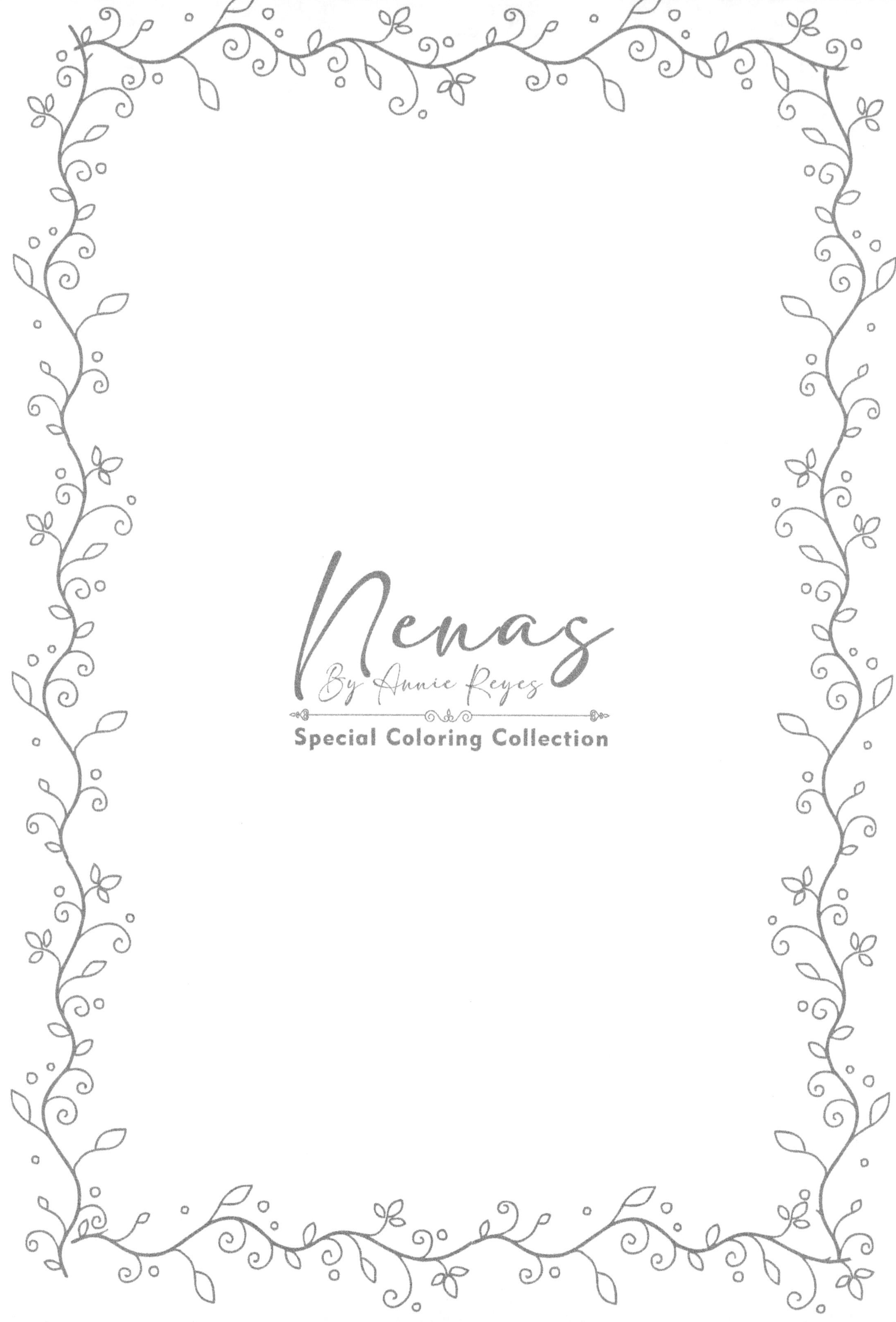
Nenas
By Annie Reyes
Special Coloring Collection

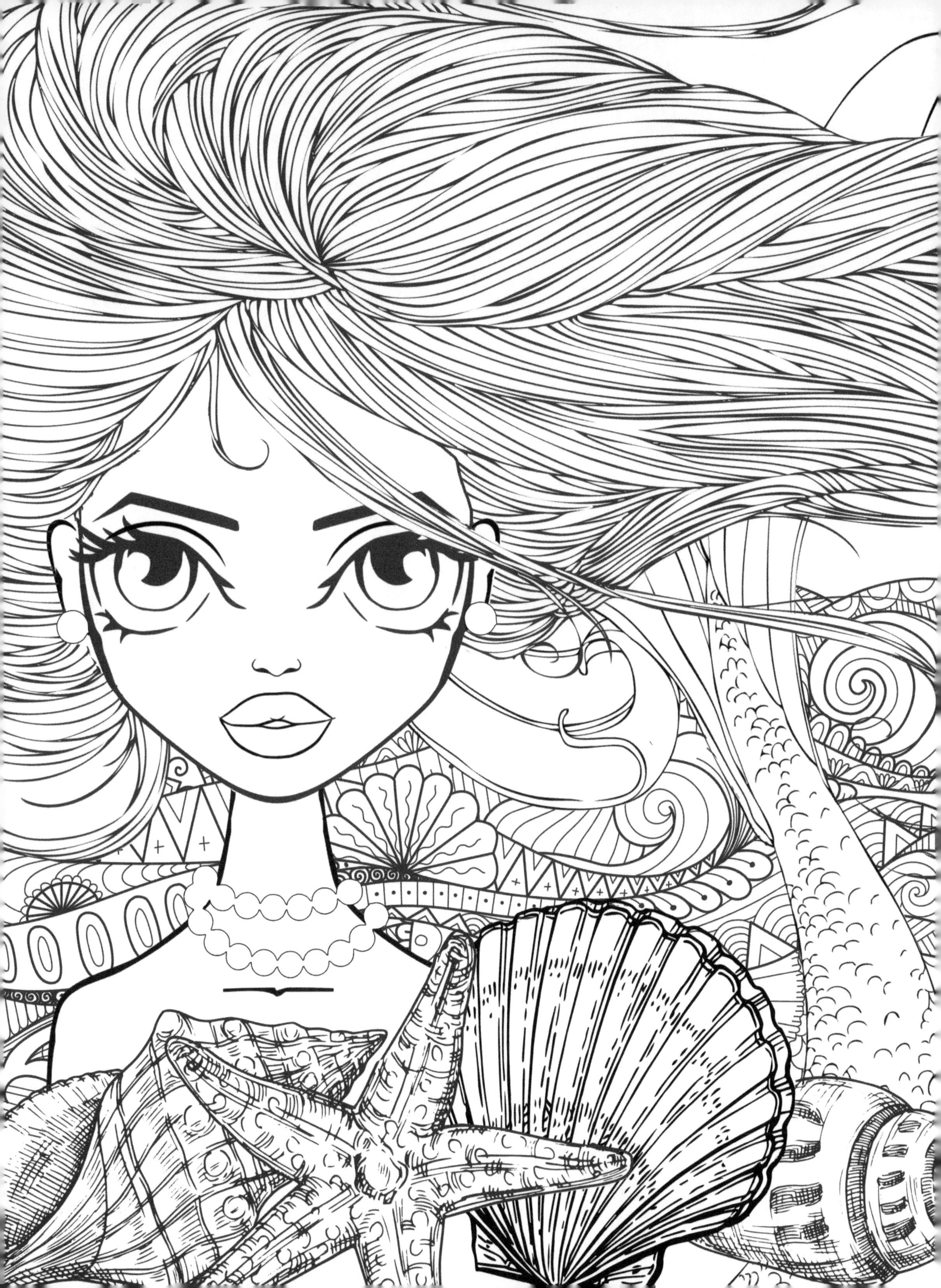

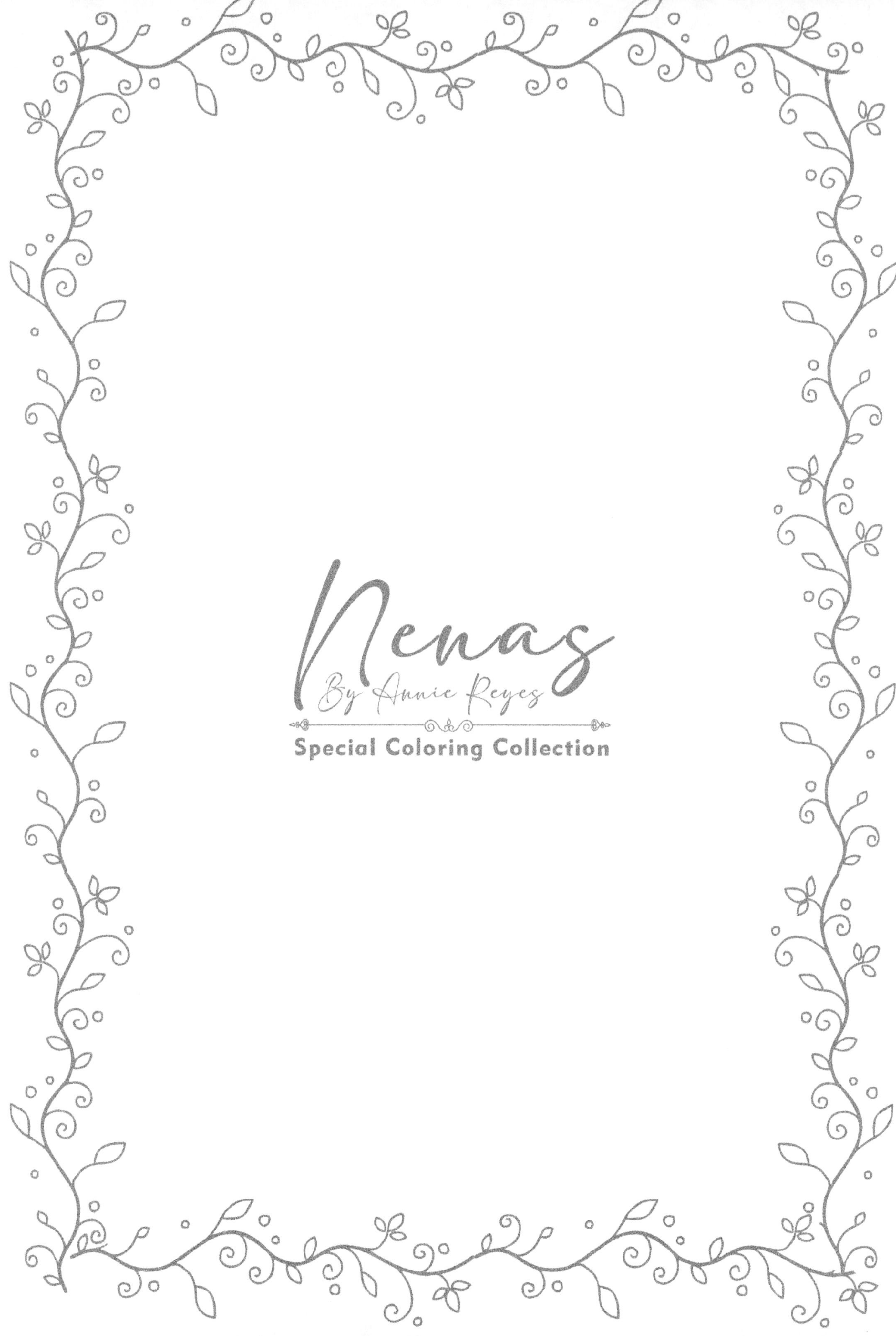

Nenas
By Annie Reyes
Special Coloring Collection

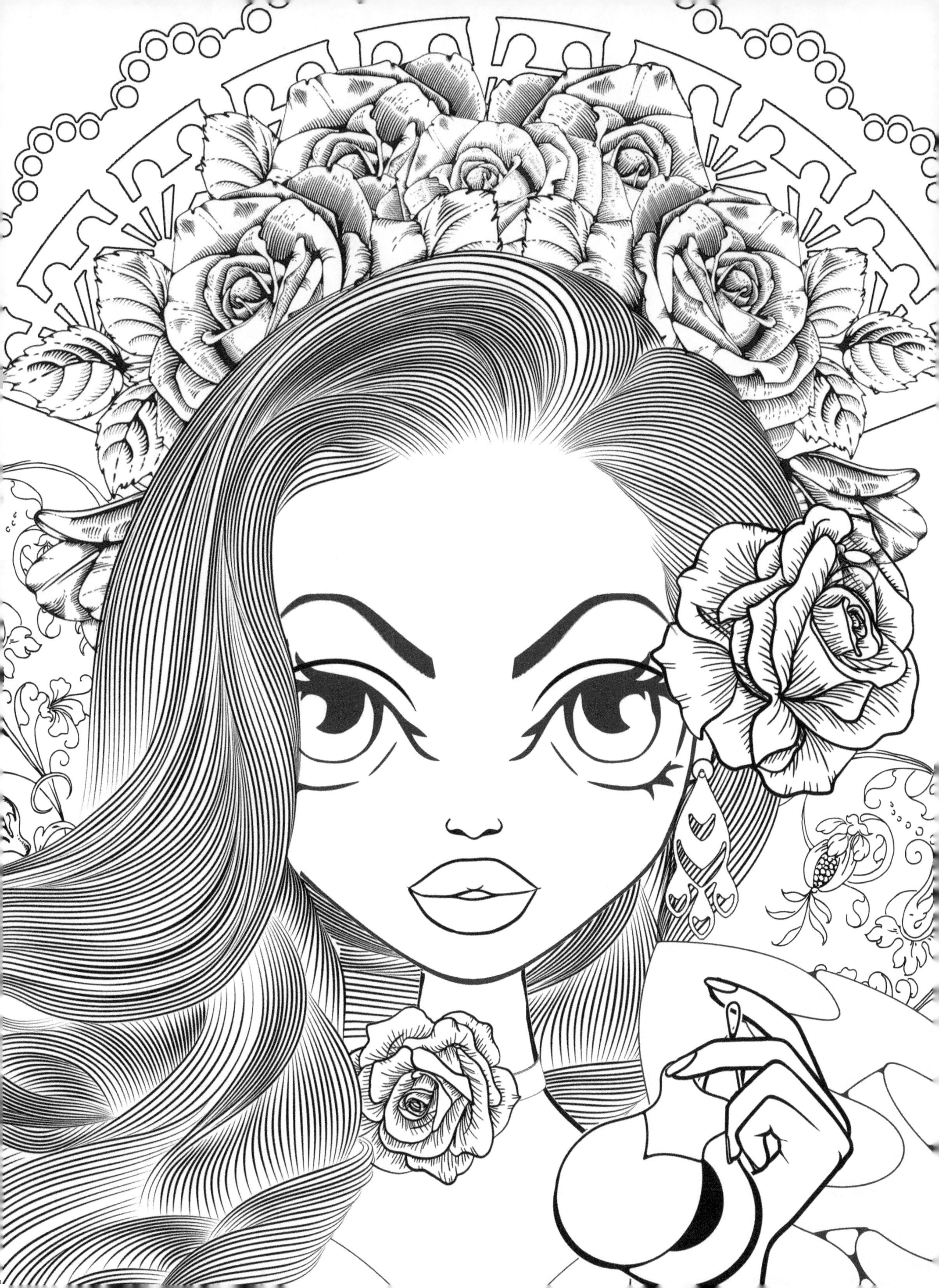

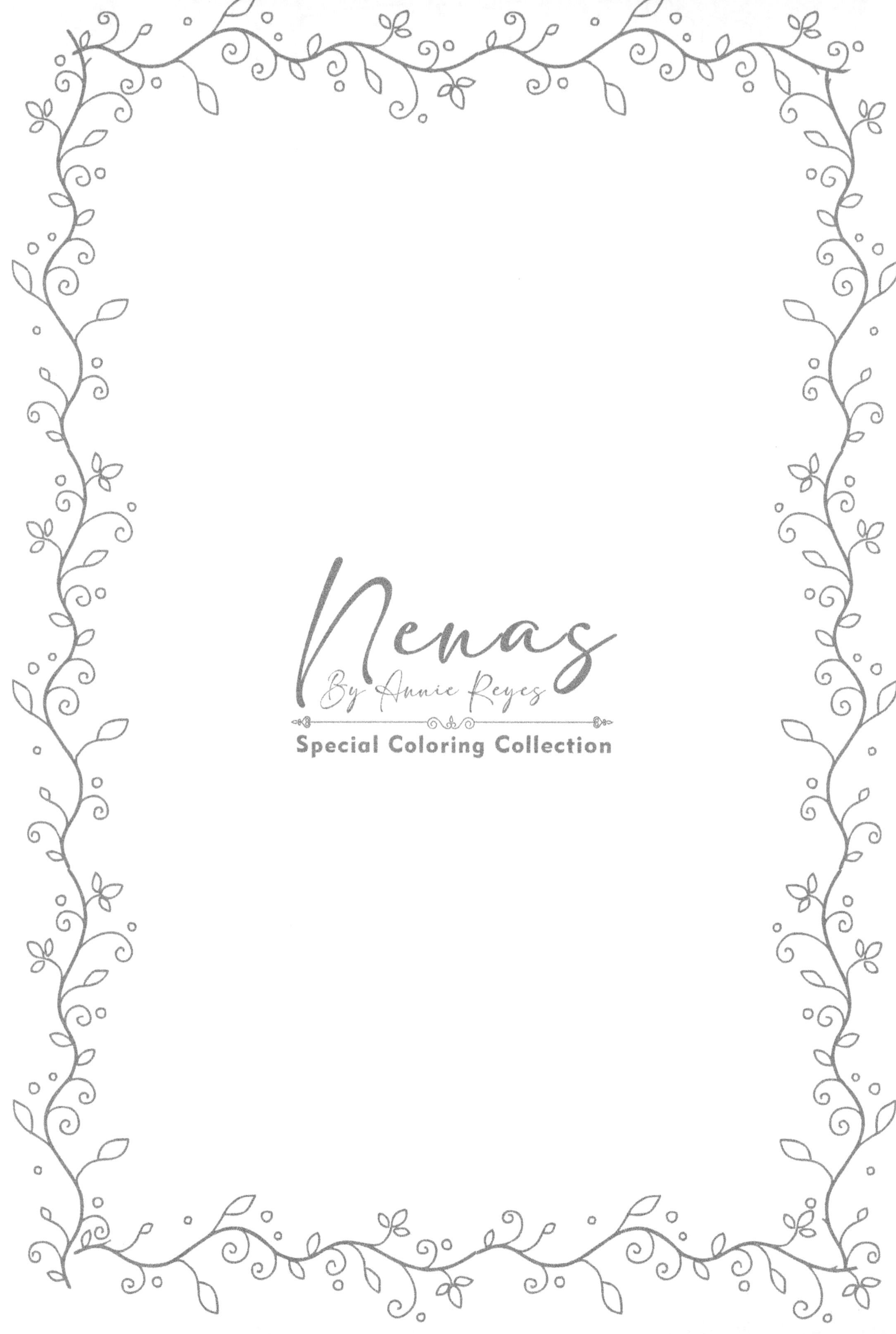

Nenas
By Annie Reyes
Special Coloring Collection

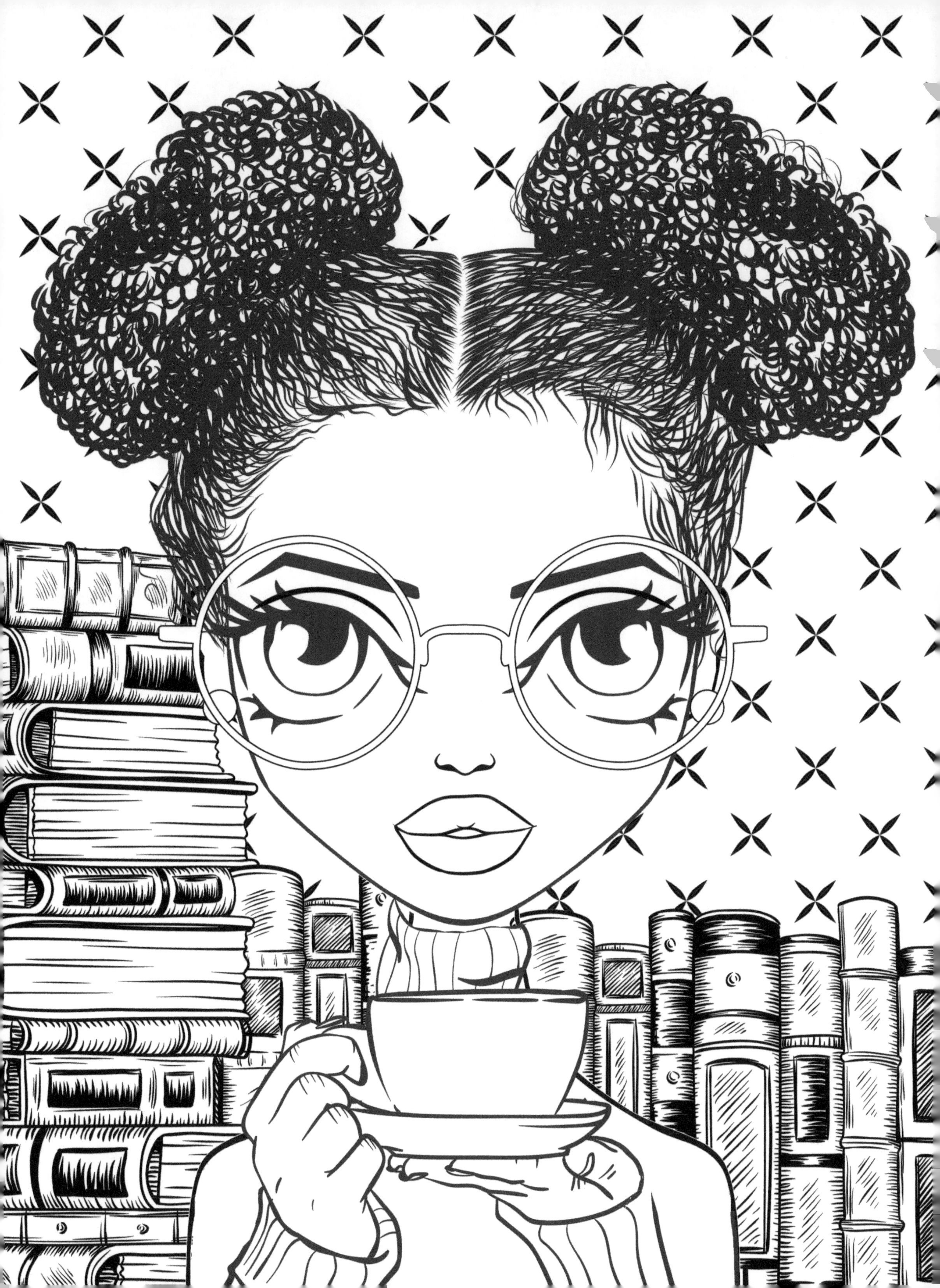

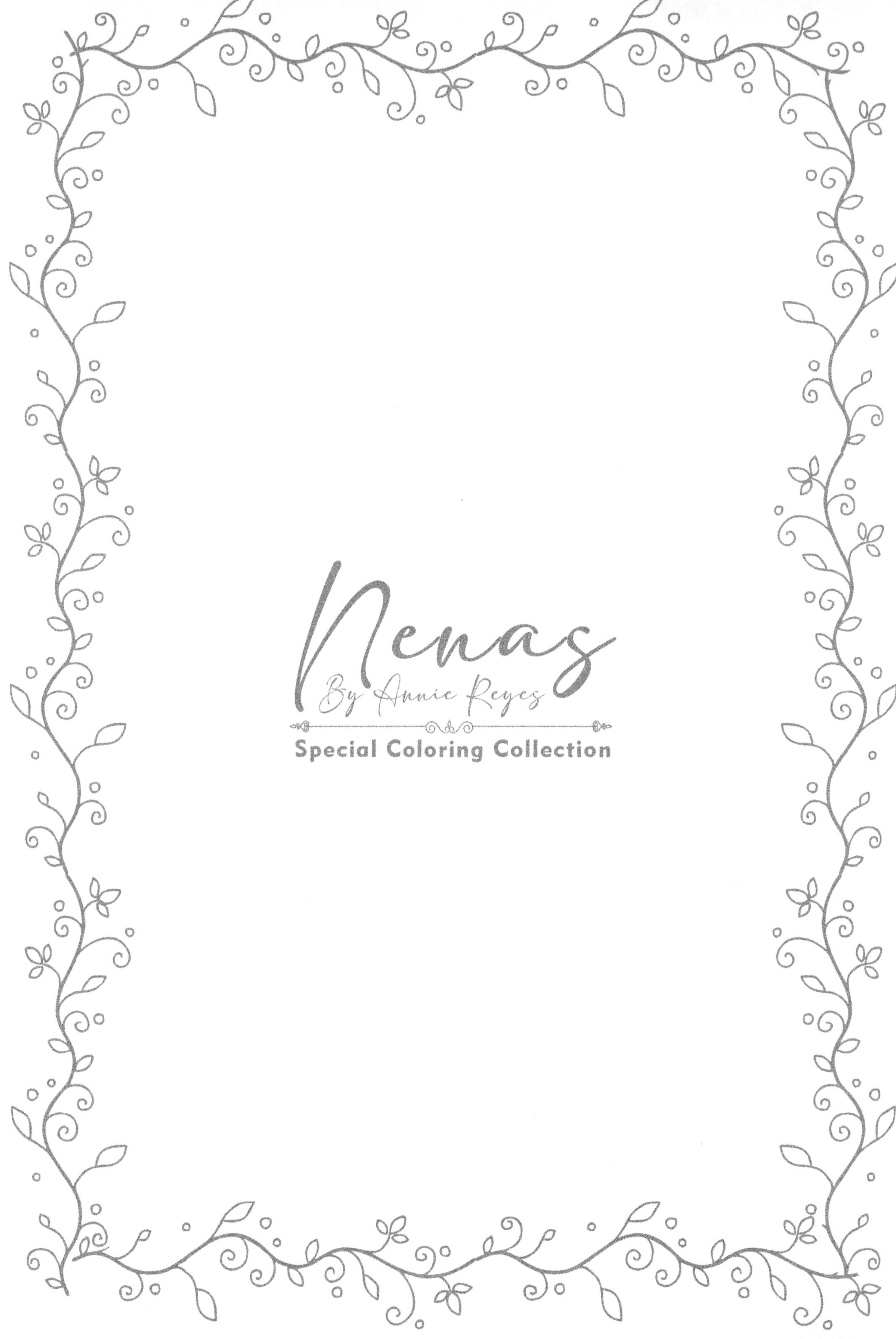
Nenas
By Annie Reyes
Special Coloring Collection

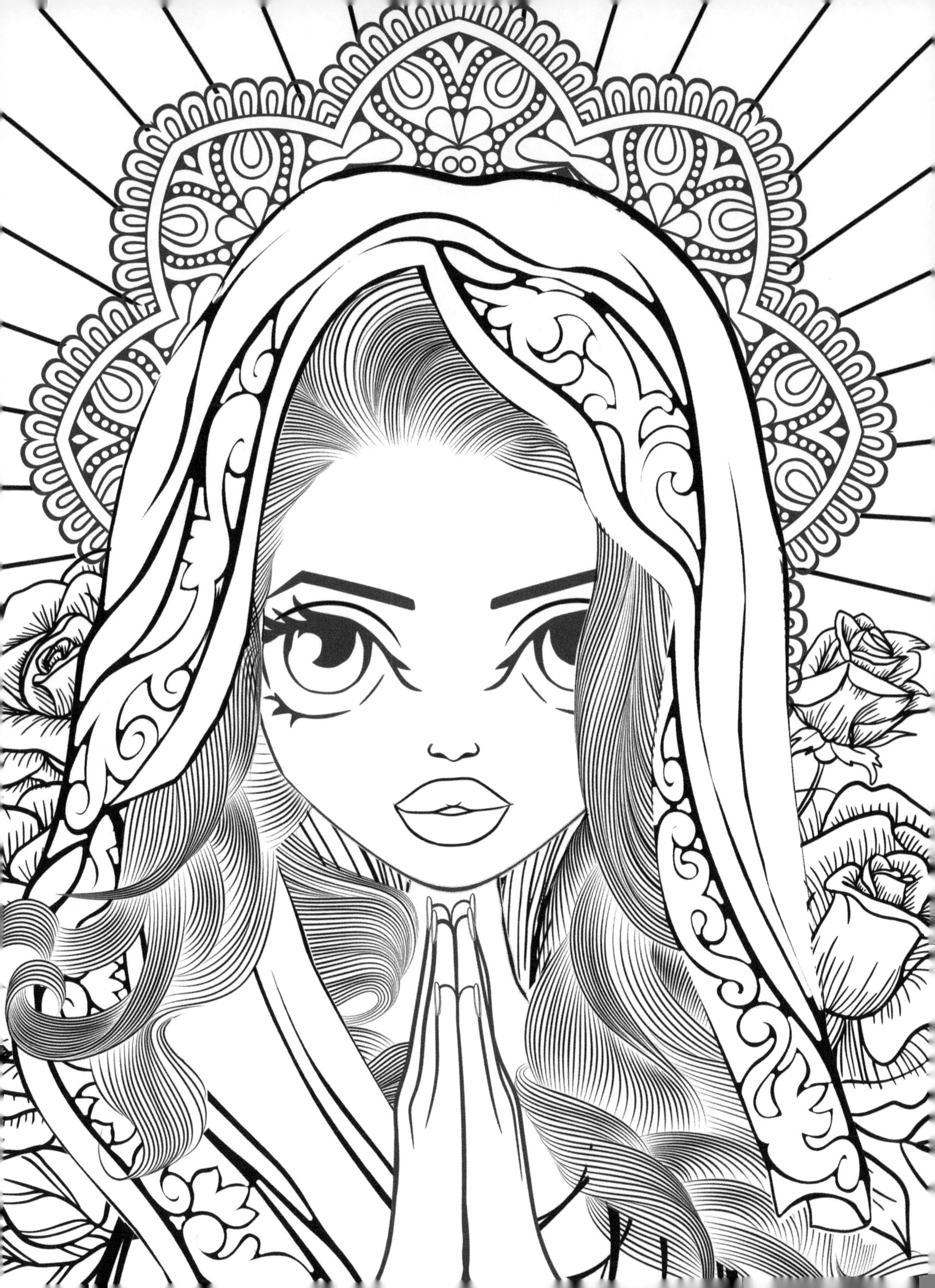

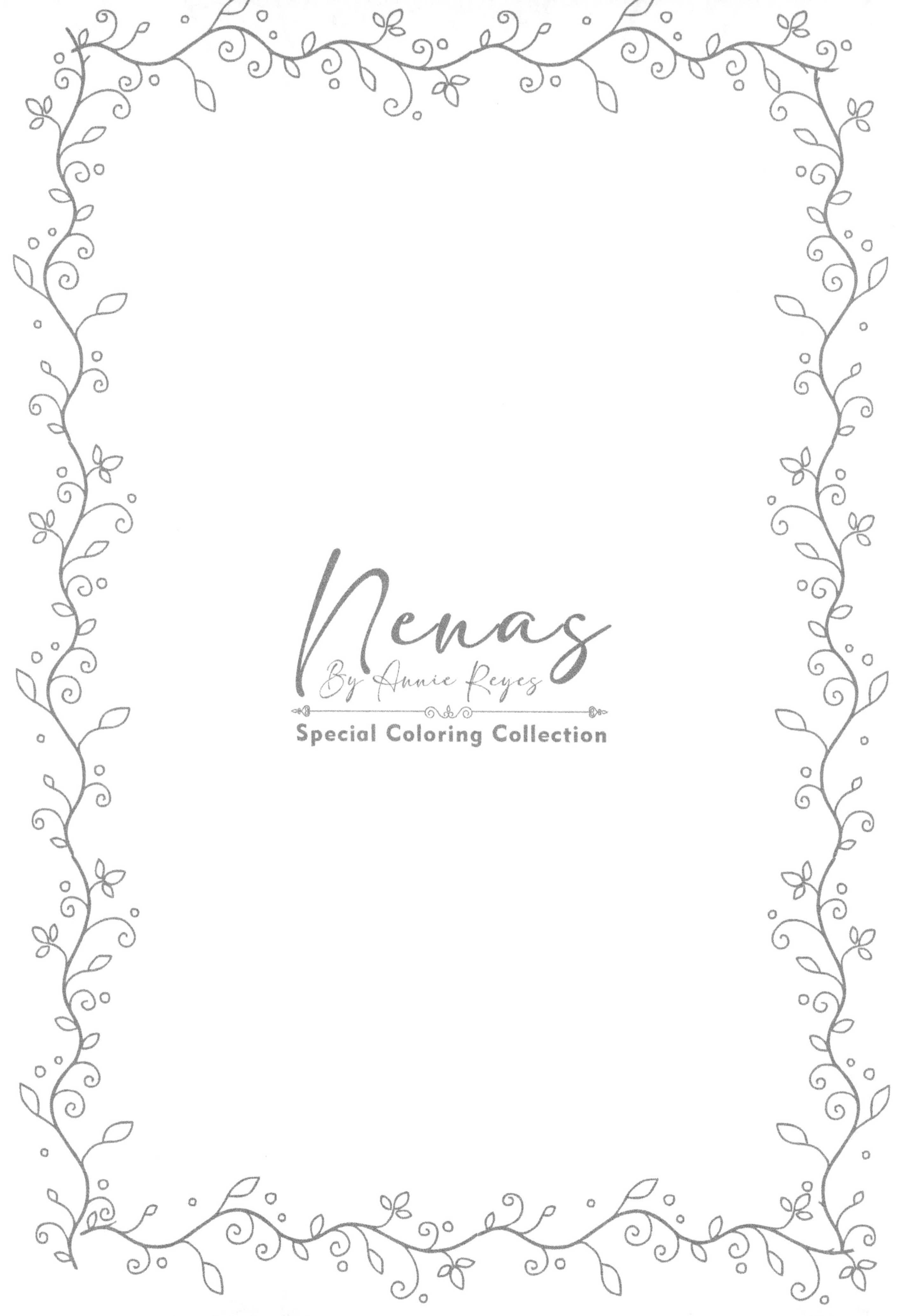

Nenas
By Annie Reyes
Special Coloring Collection

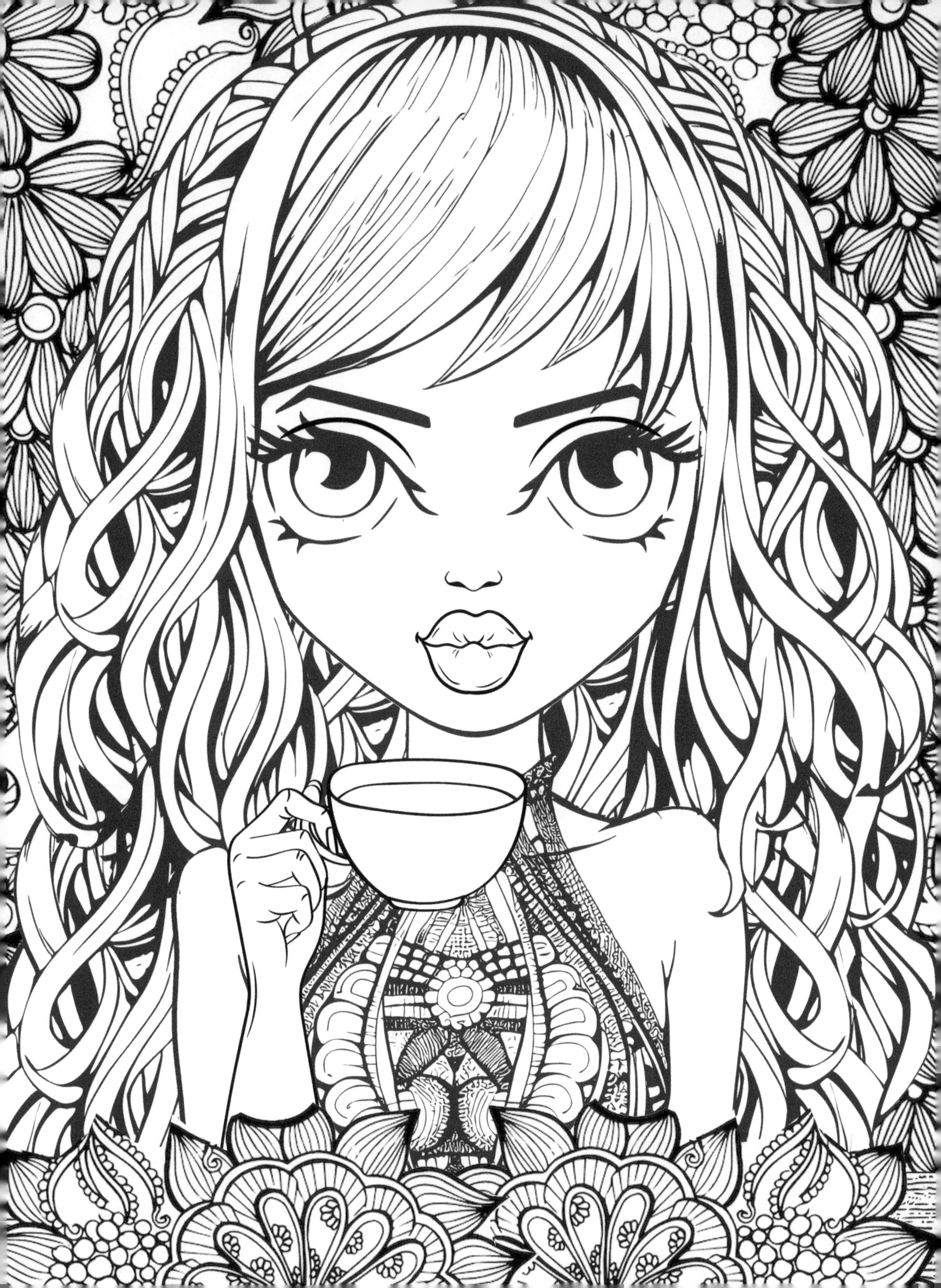

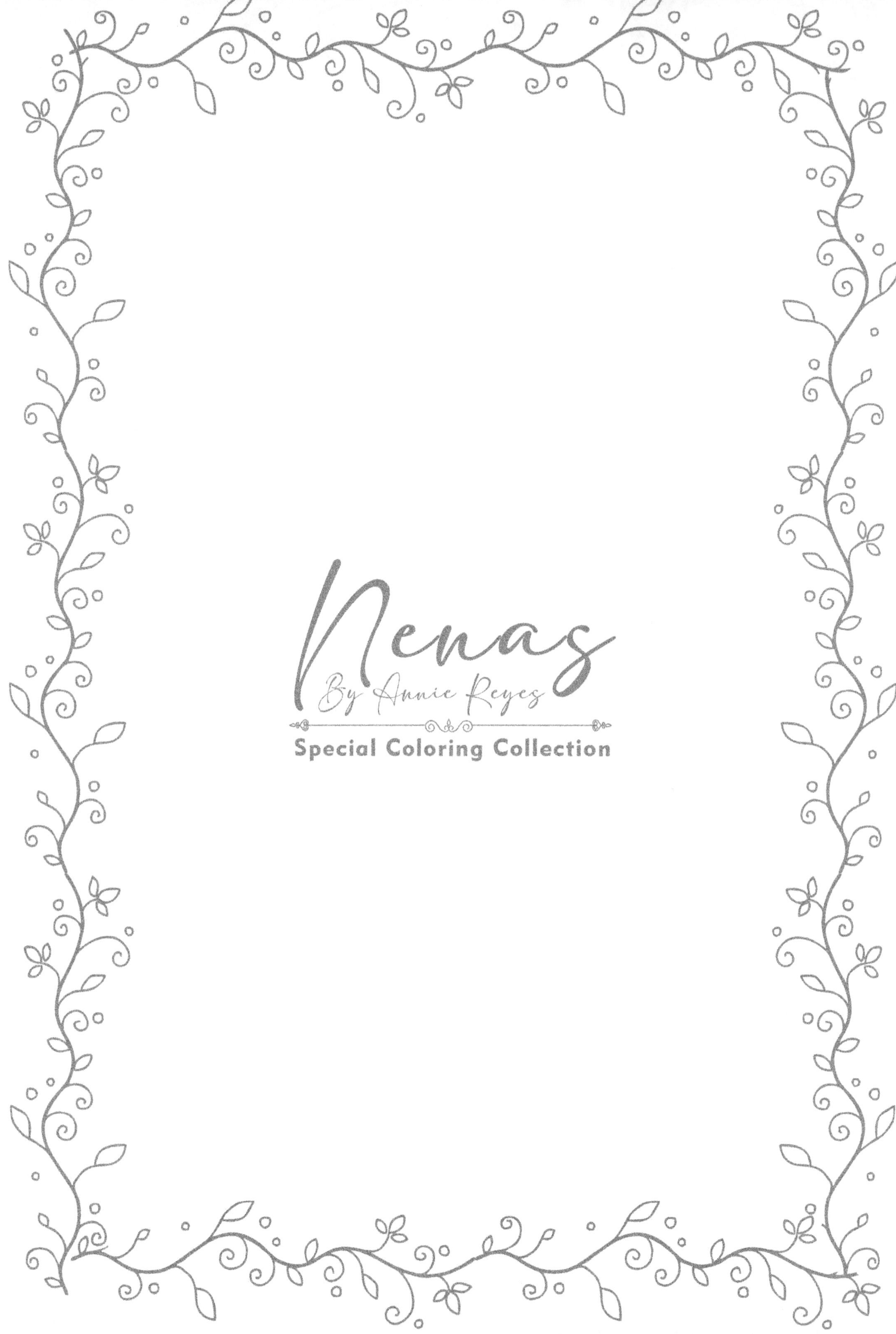

Nenas
By Annie Reyes
Special Coloring Collection

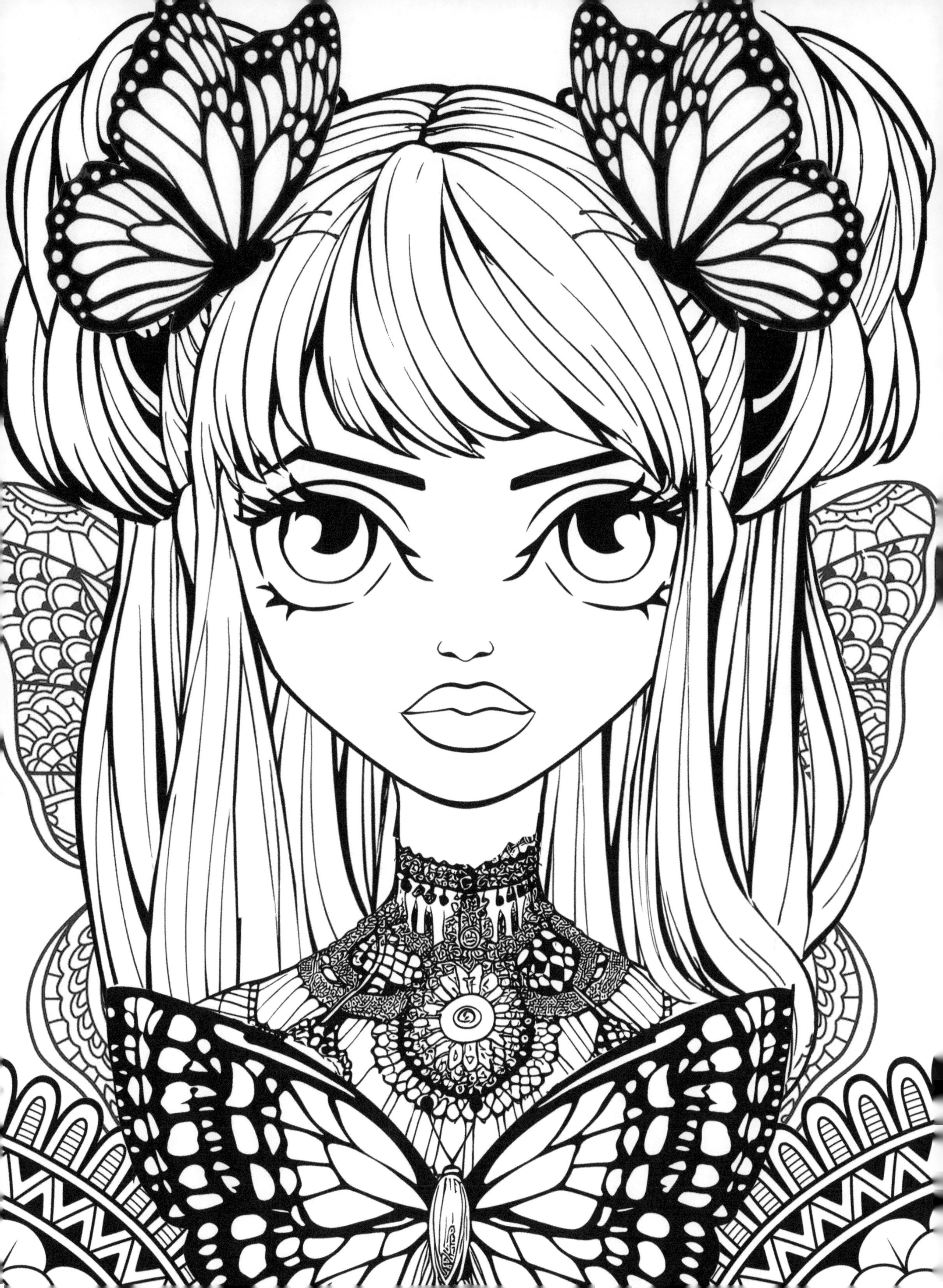

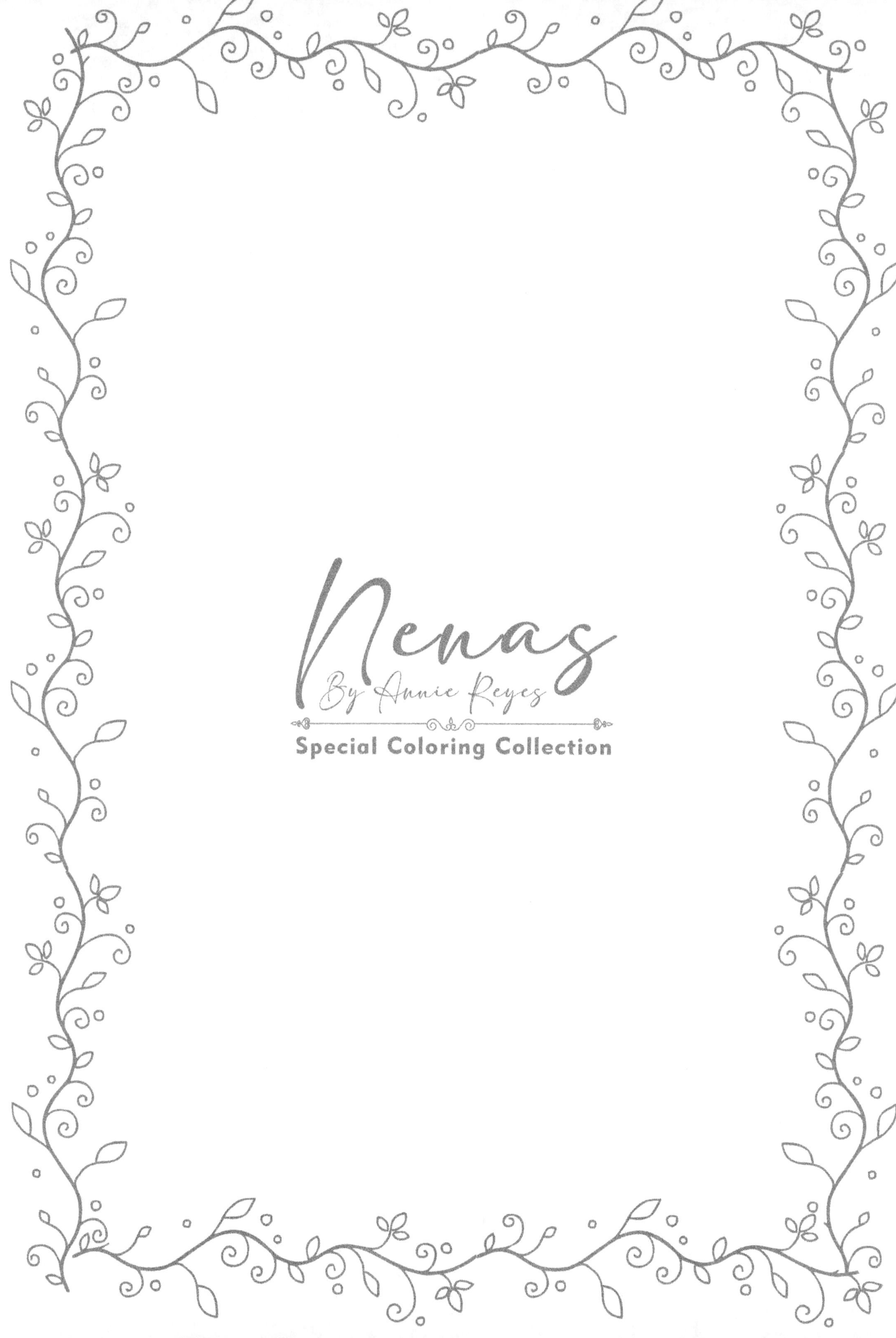

Nenas
By Annie Reyes
Special Coloring Collection

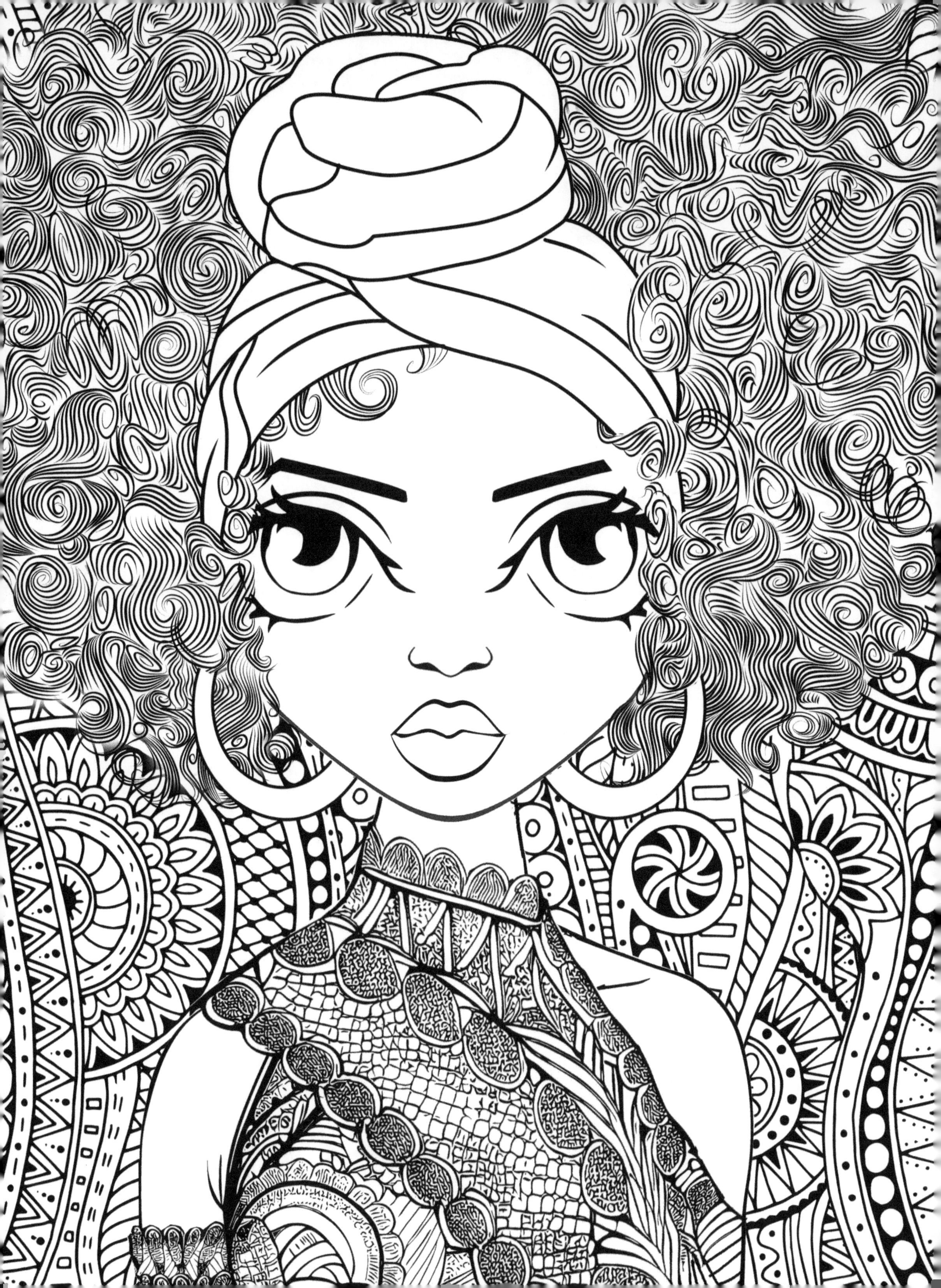

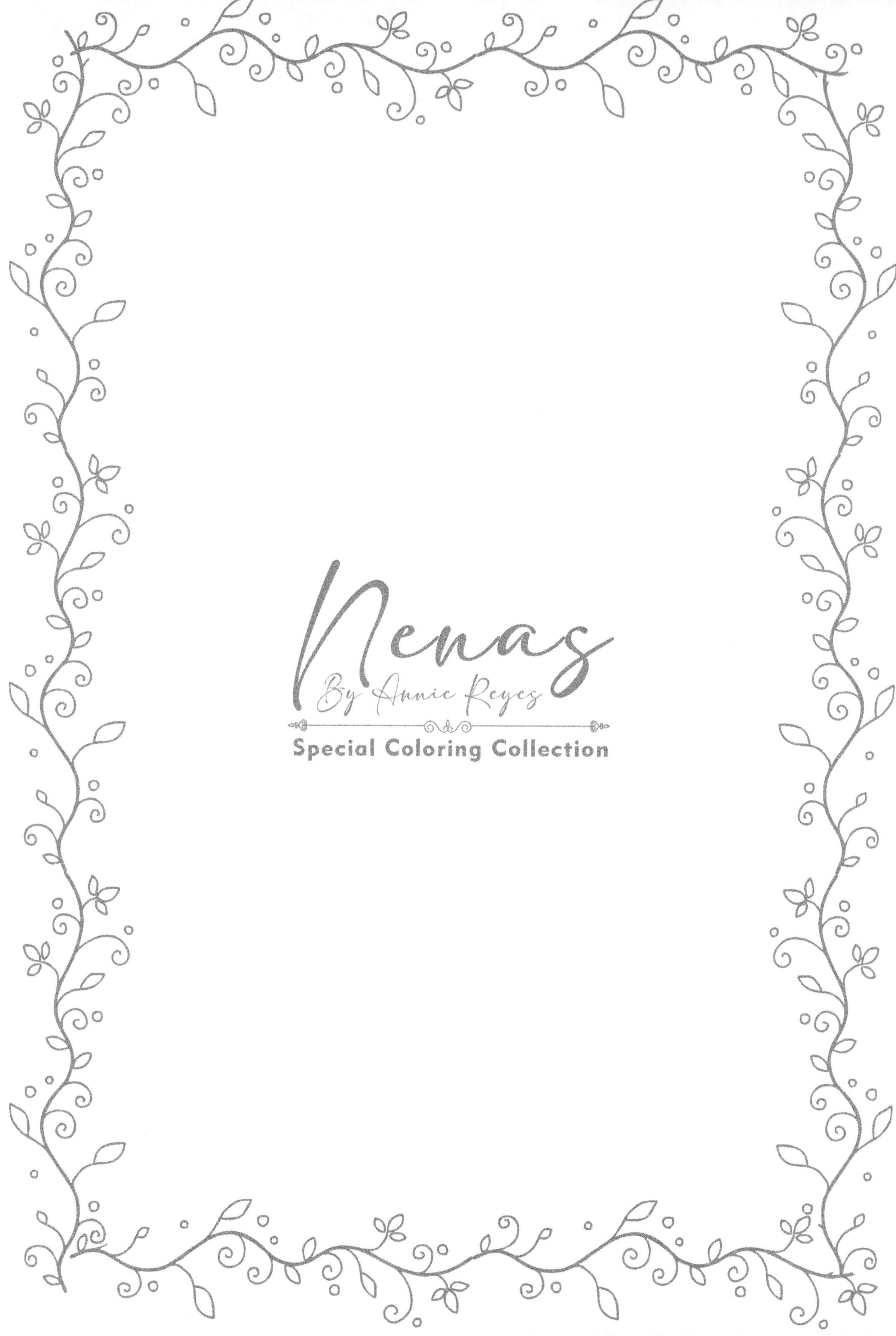

Nenas
By Annie Reyes
Special Coloring Collection

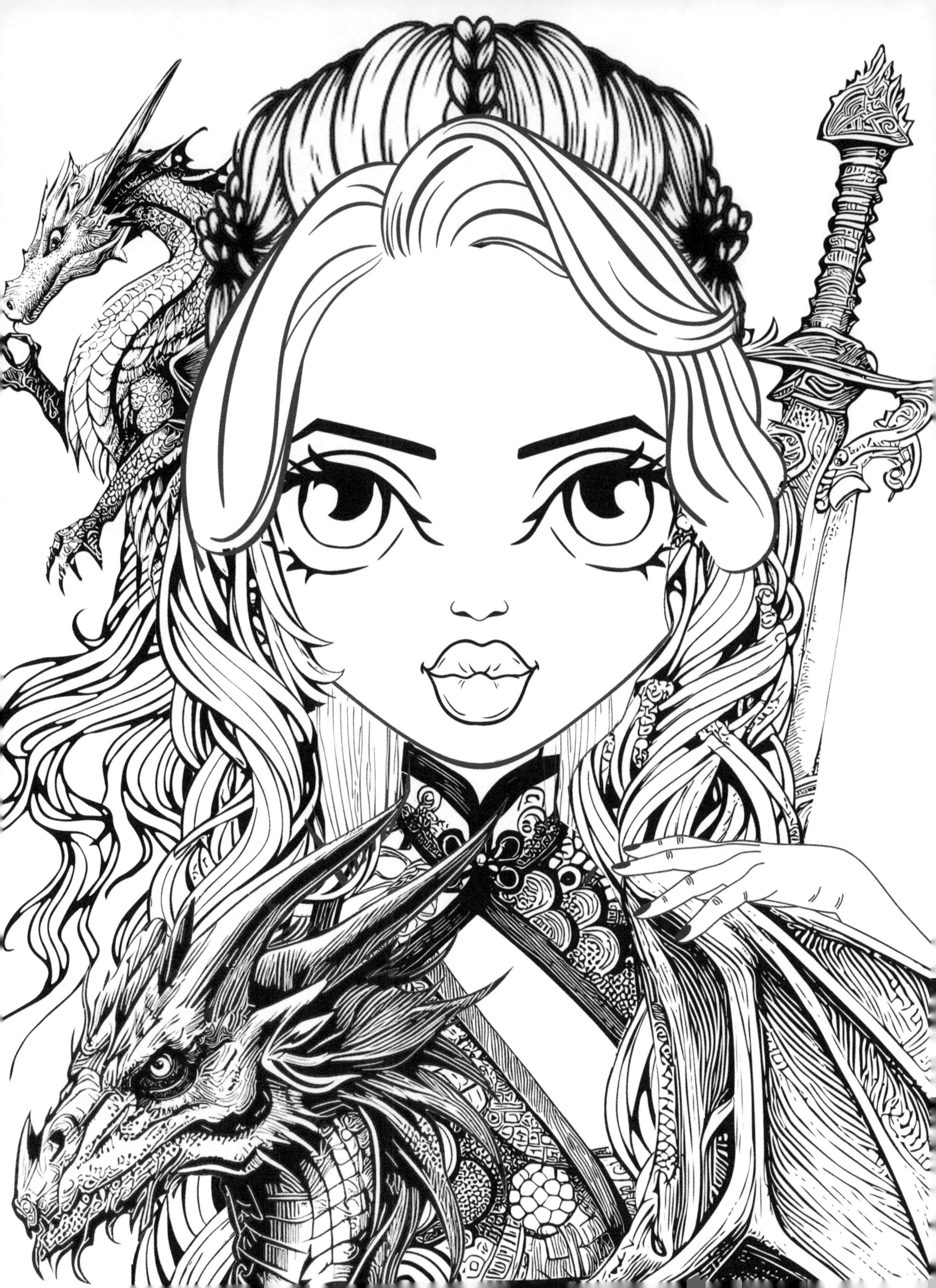

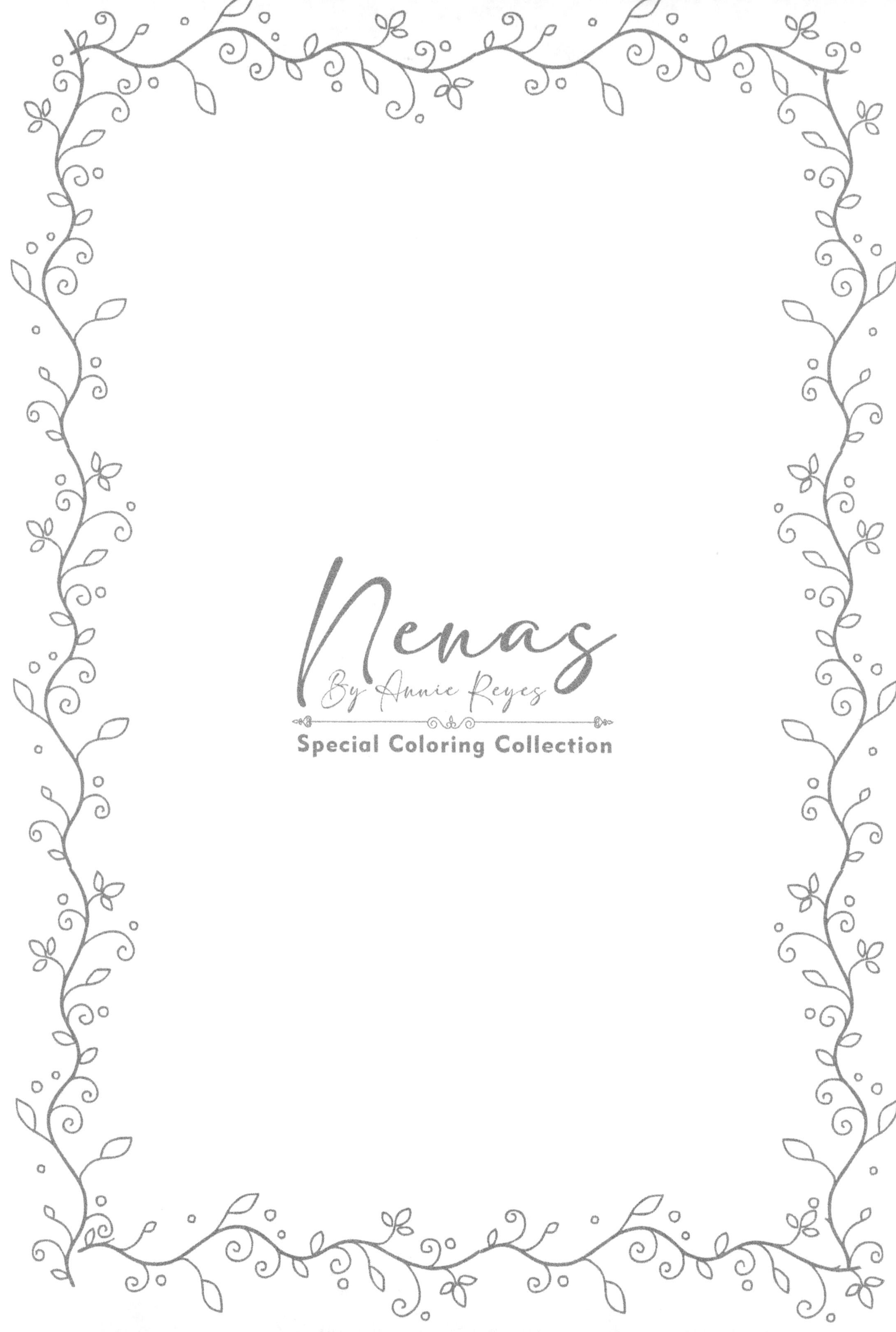

Nenas
By Annie Reyes
Special Coloring Collection

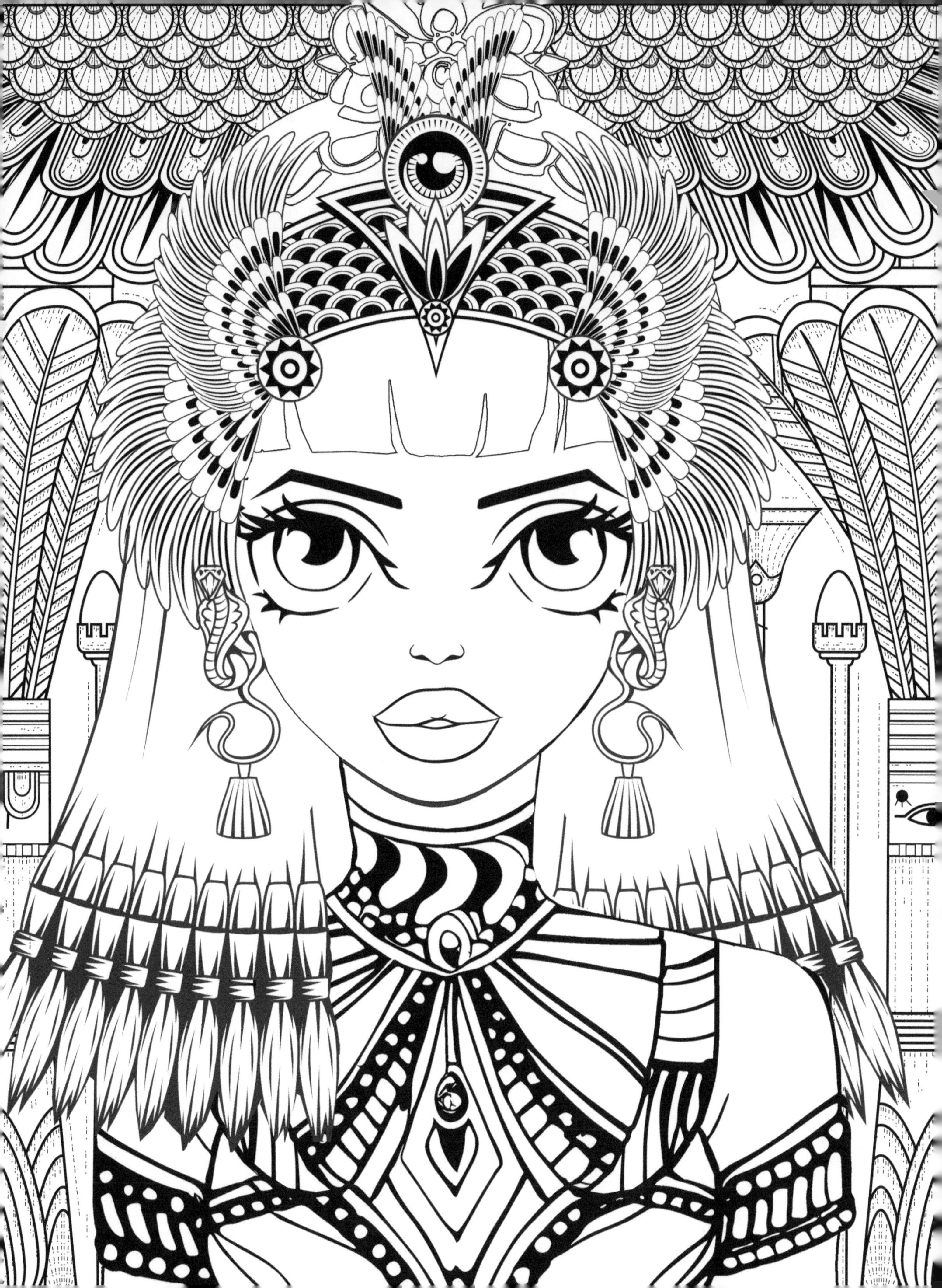

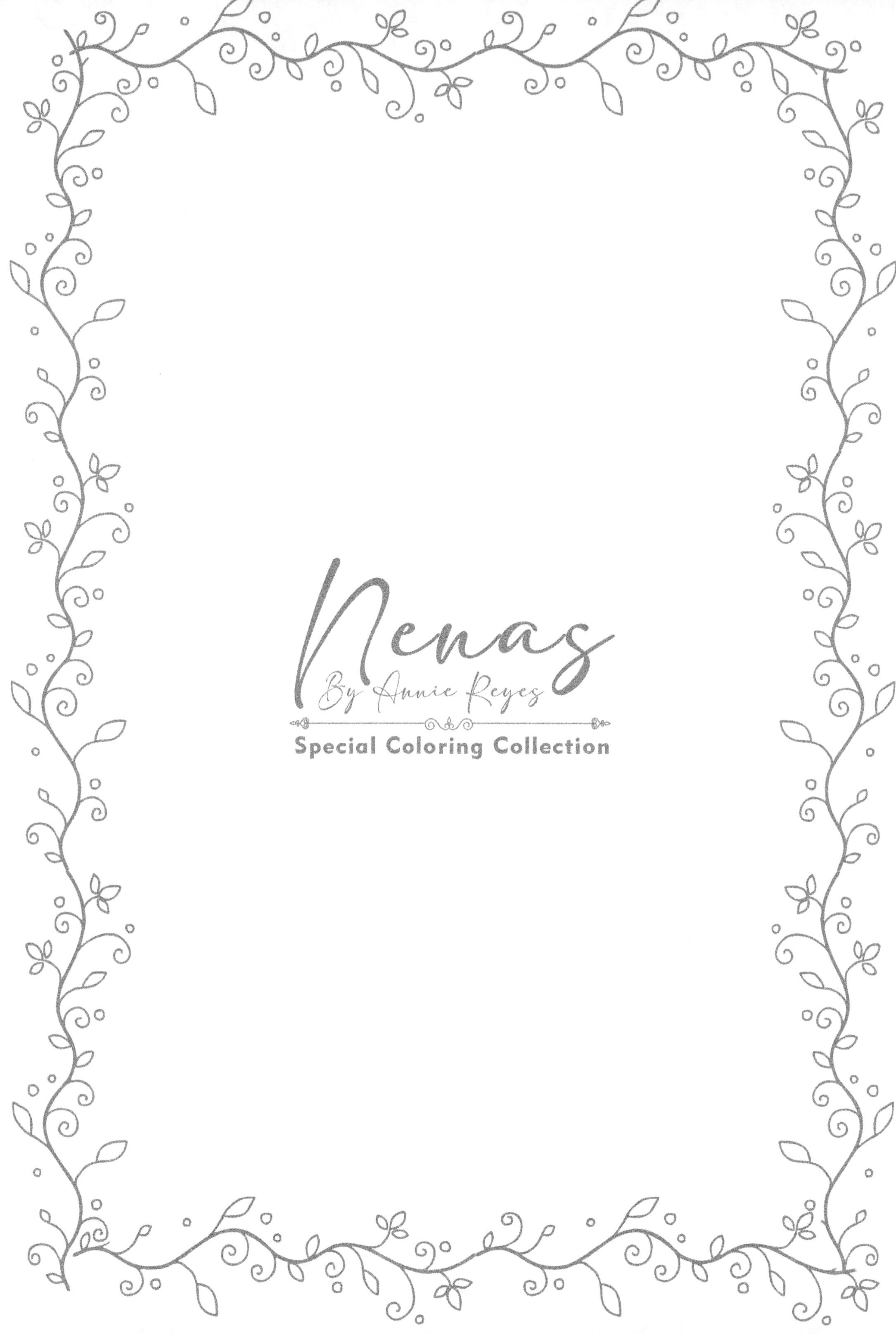

Nenas
By Annie Reyes
Special Coloring Collection

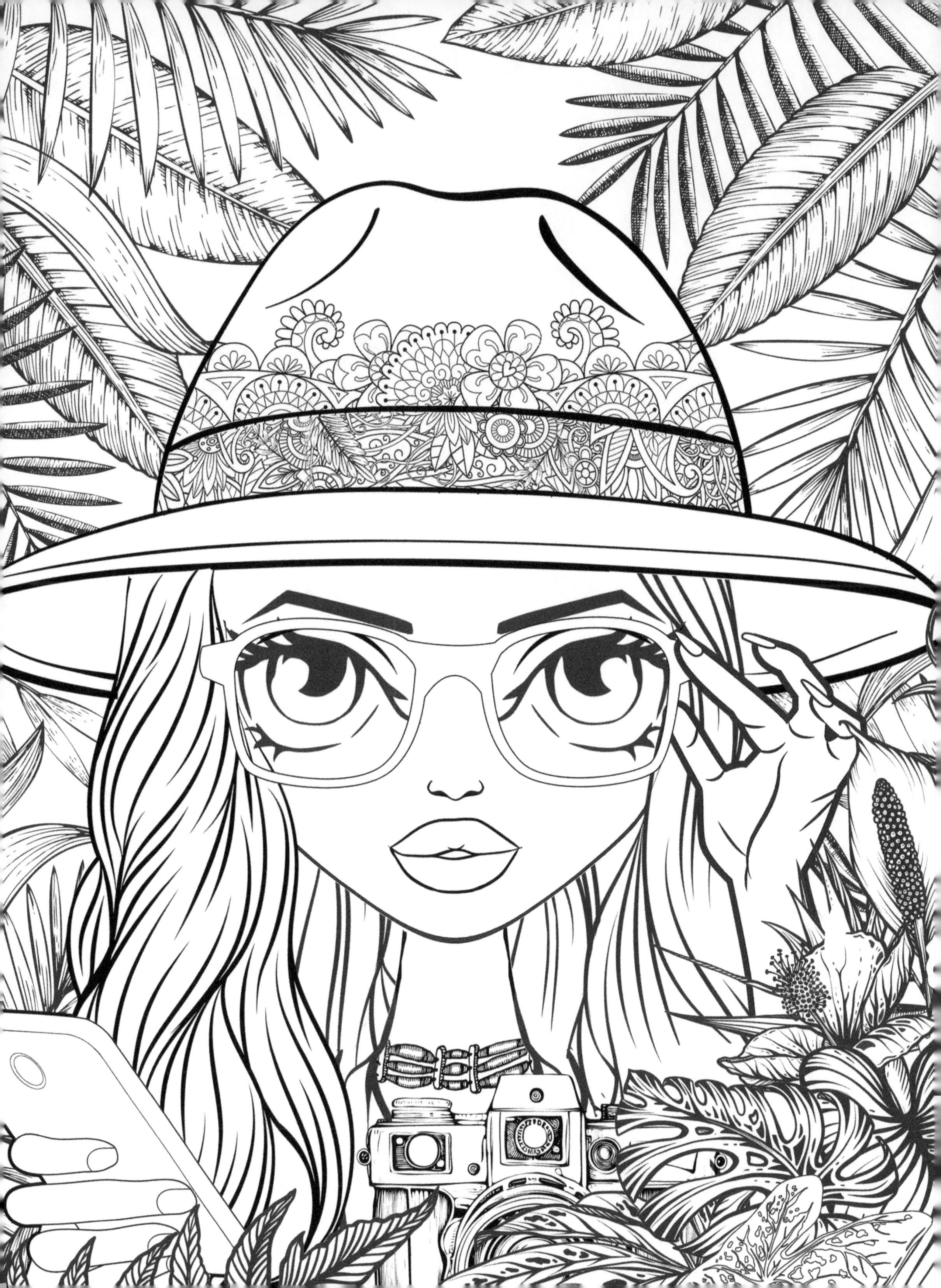

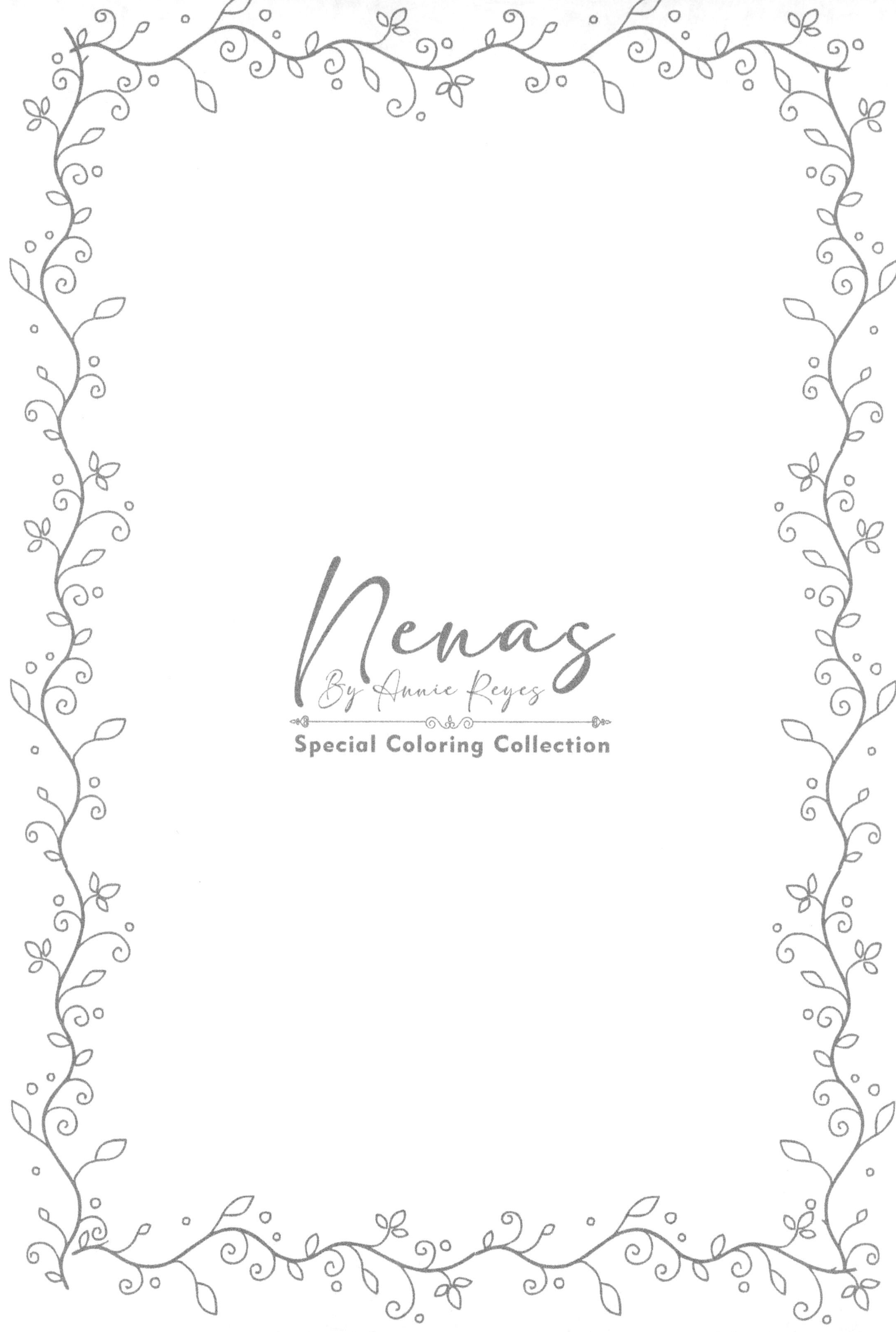

Nenas
By Annie Reyes
Special Coloring Collection

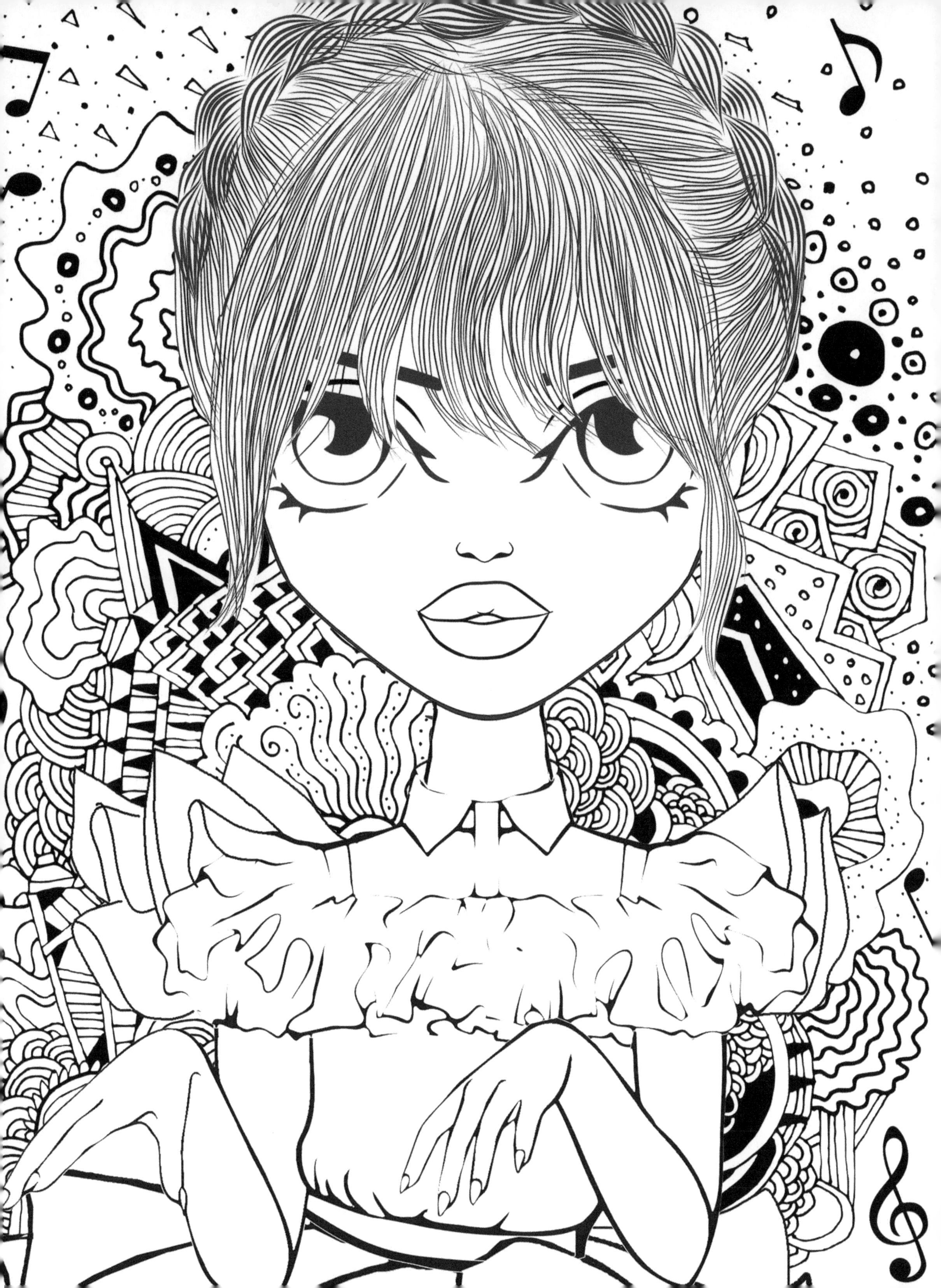

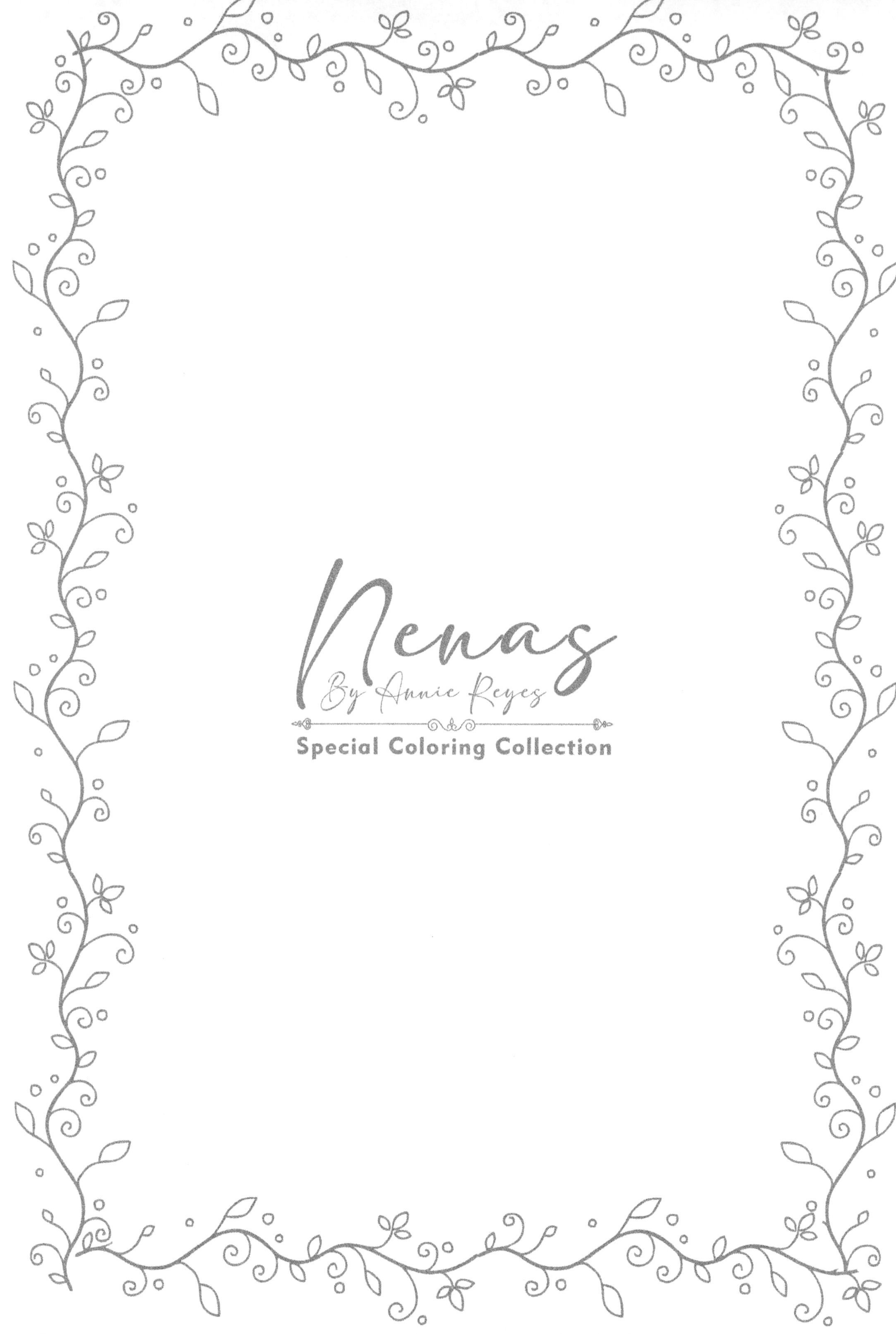

Nenas
By Annie Reyes
Special Coloring Collection

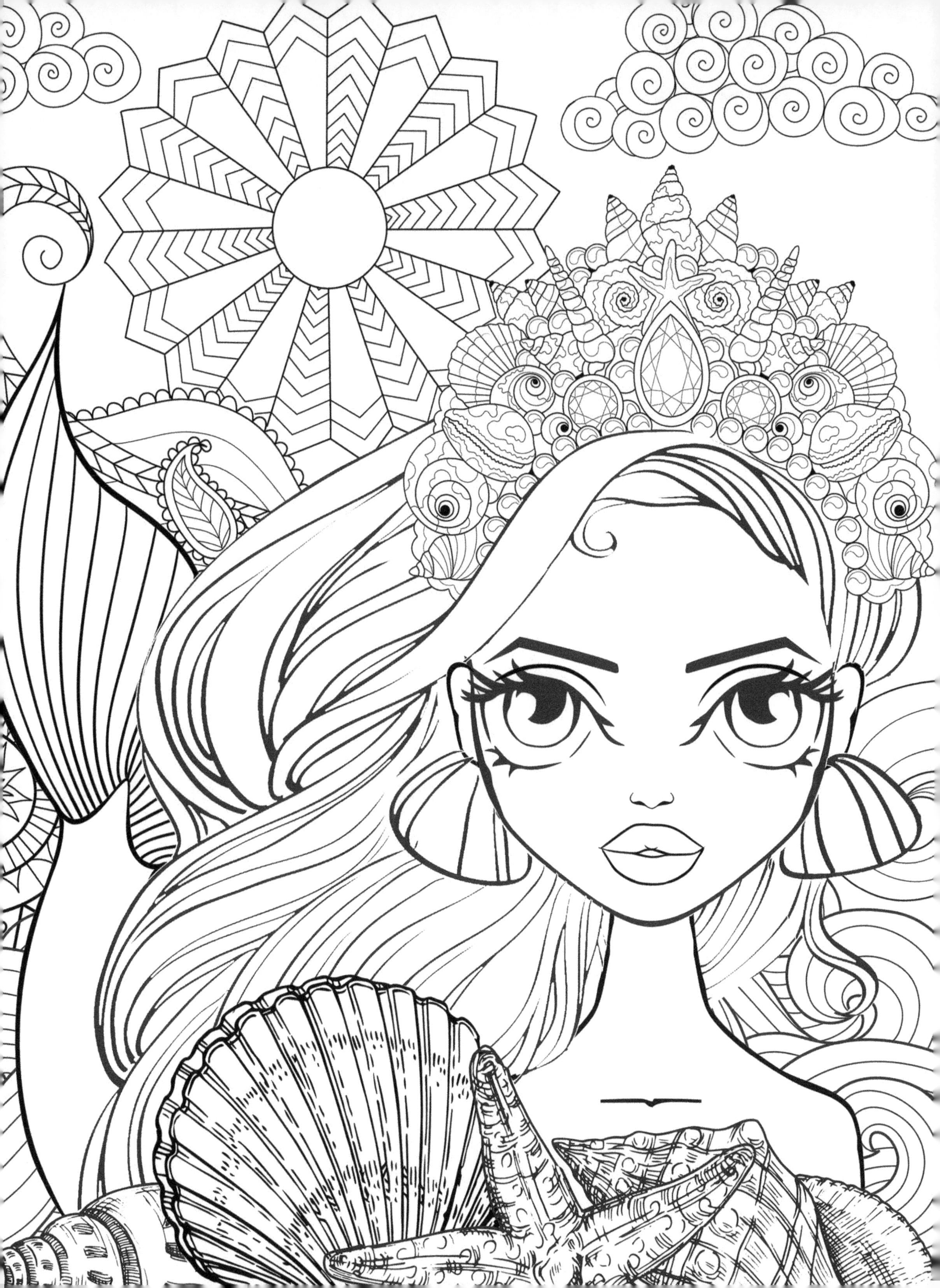

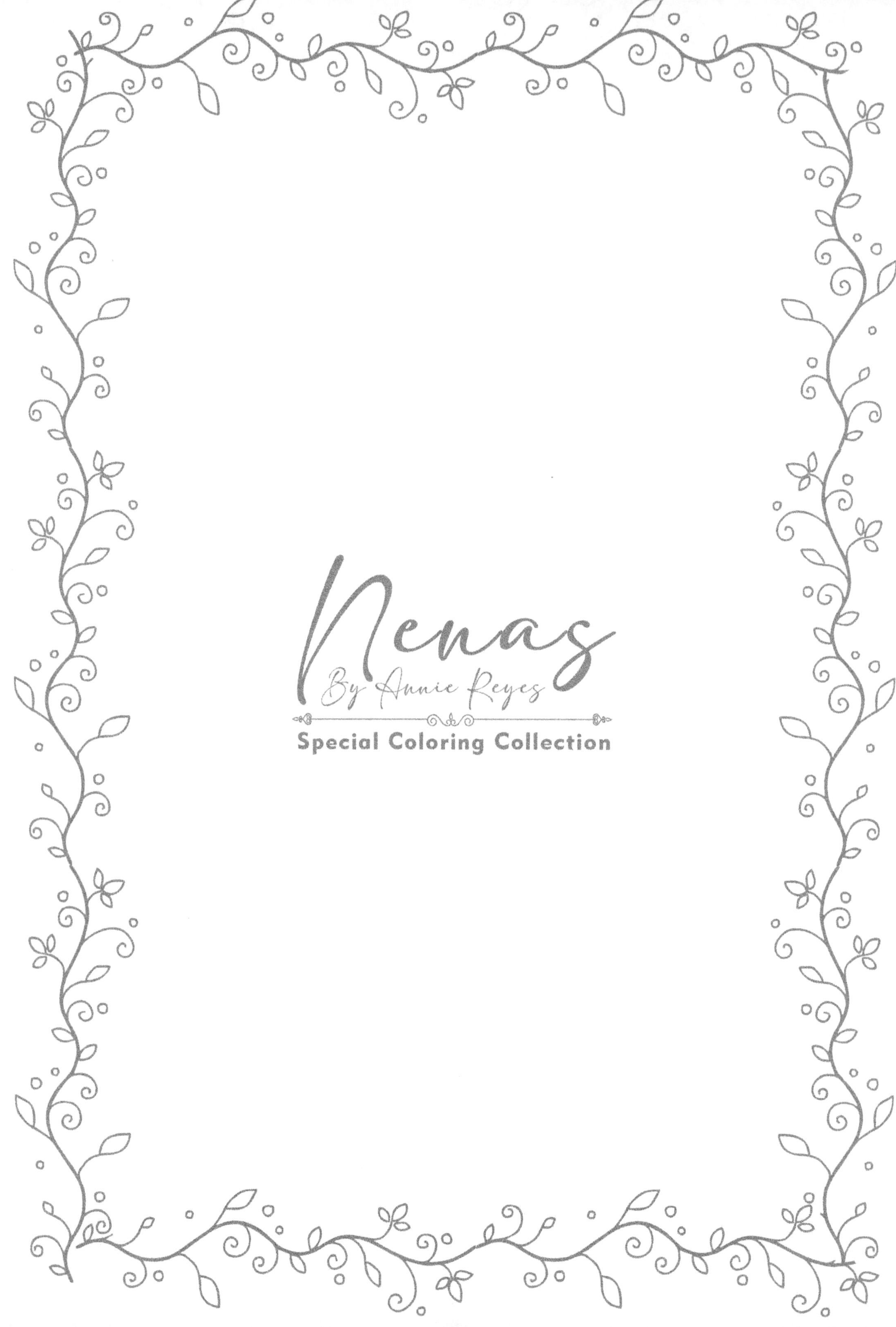

Nenas
By Annie Reyes
Special Coloring Collection

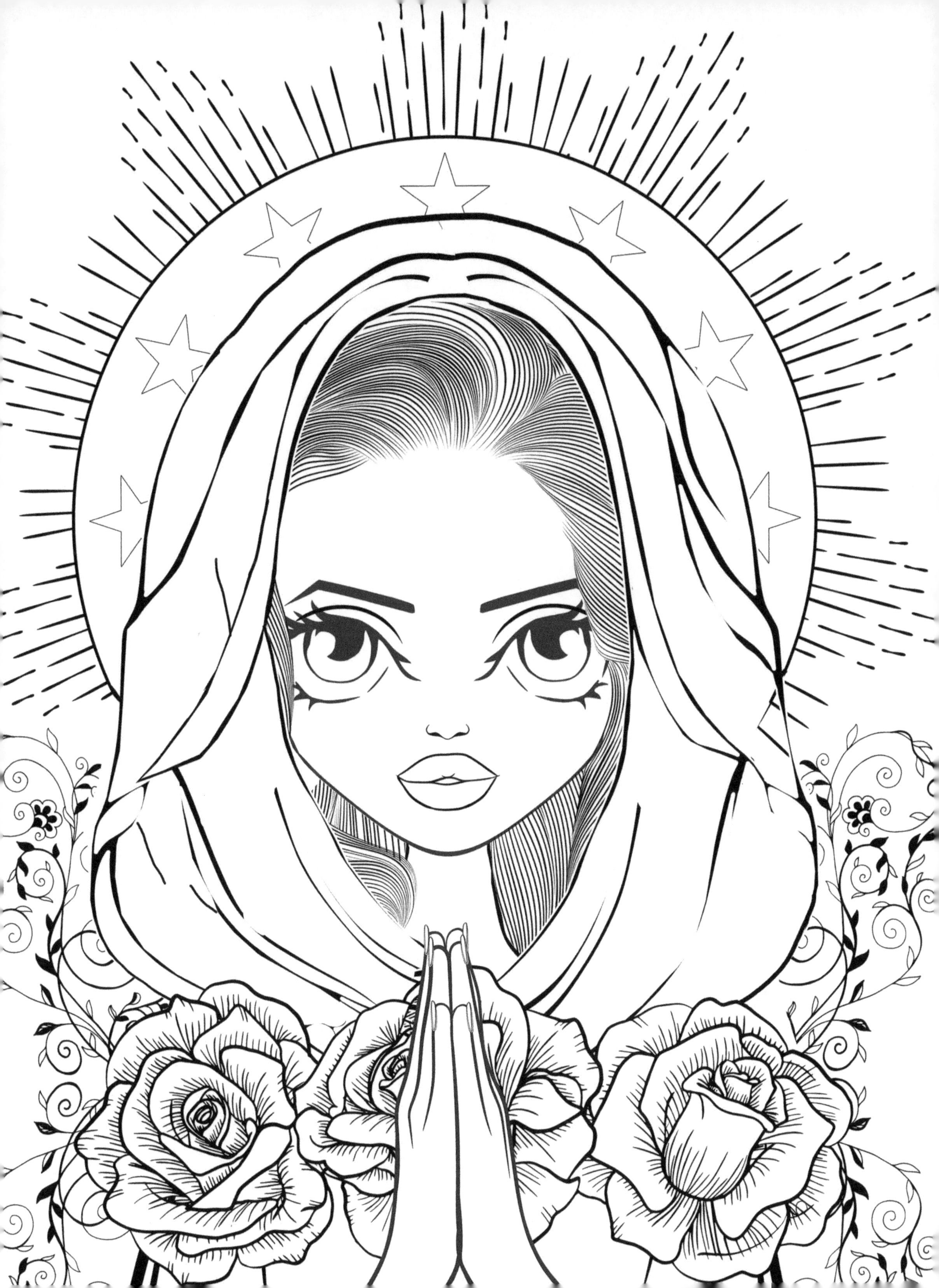

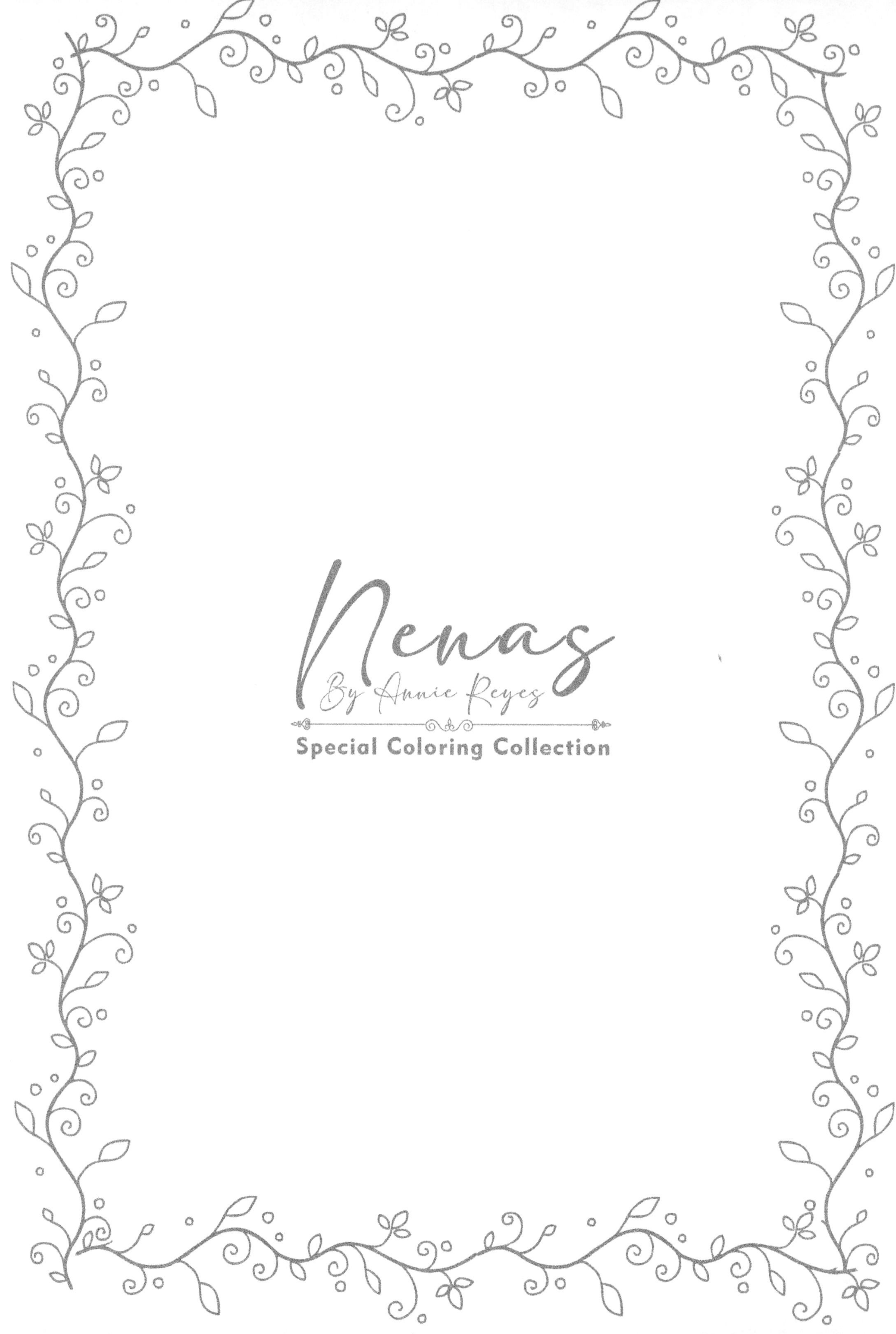
Nenas
By Annie Reyes
Special Coloring Collection

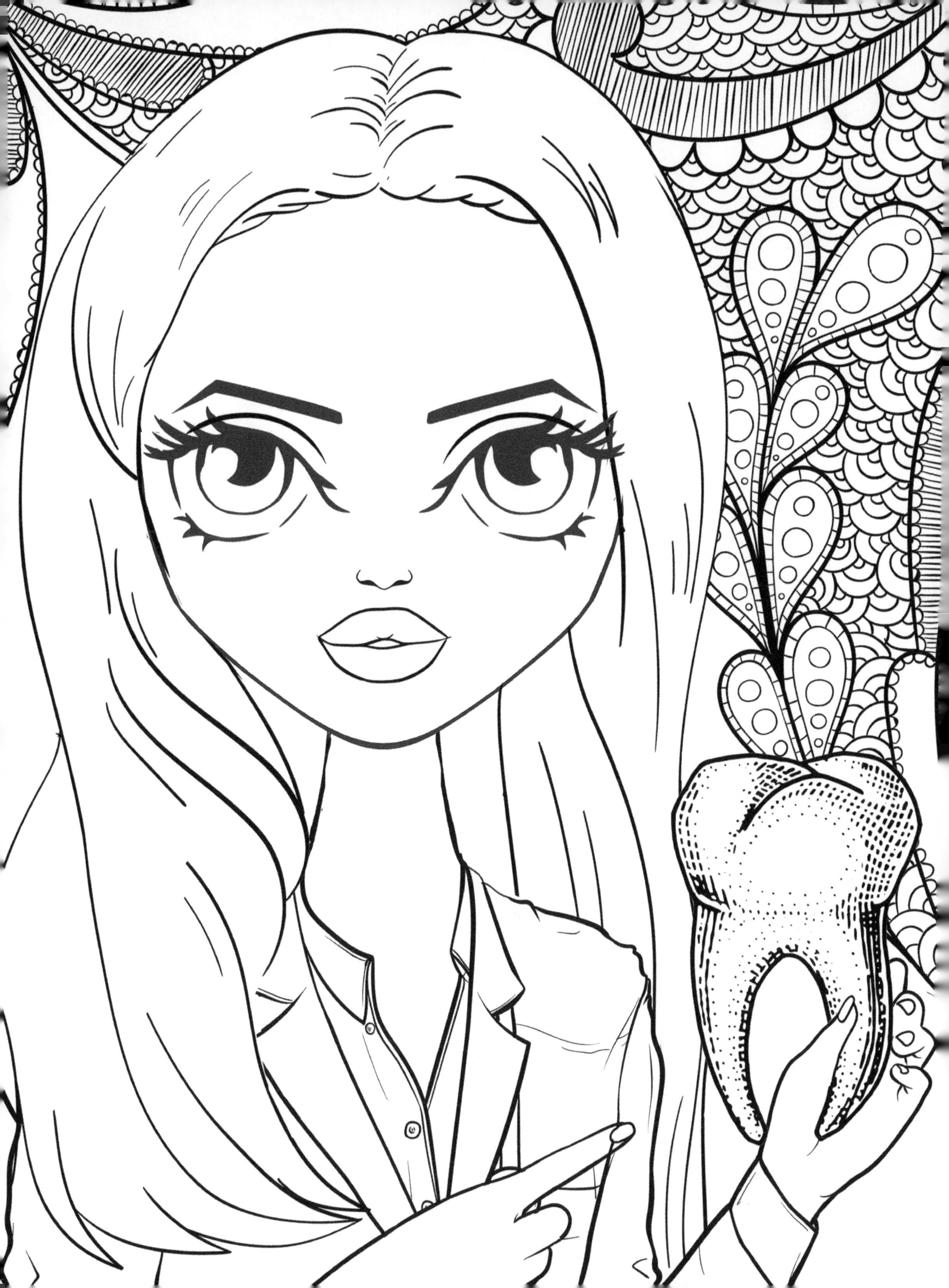

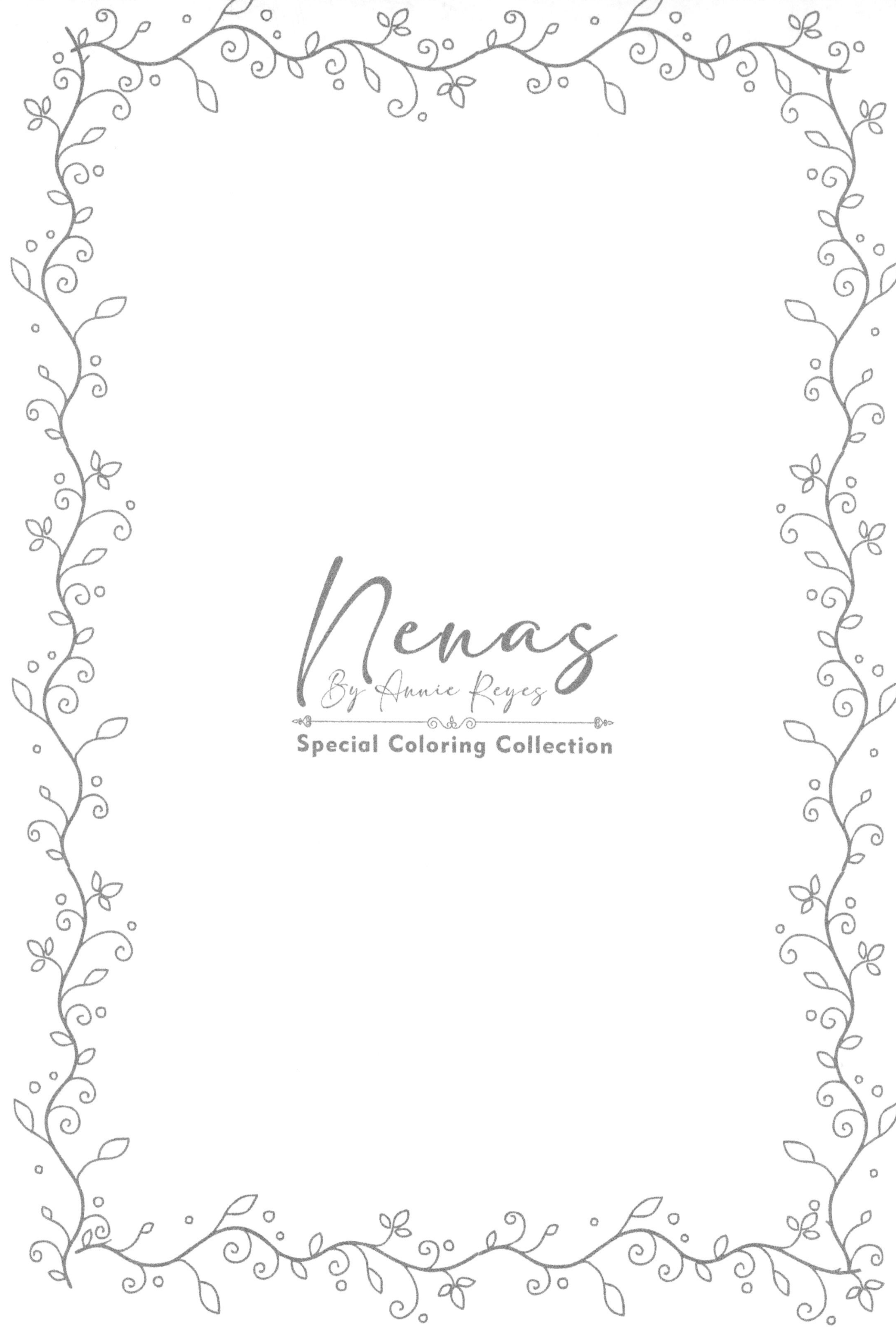

Nenas
By Annie Reyes
Special Coloring Collection

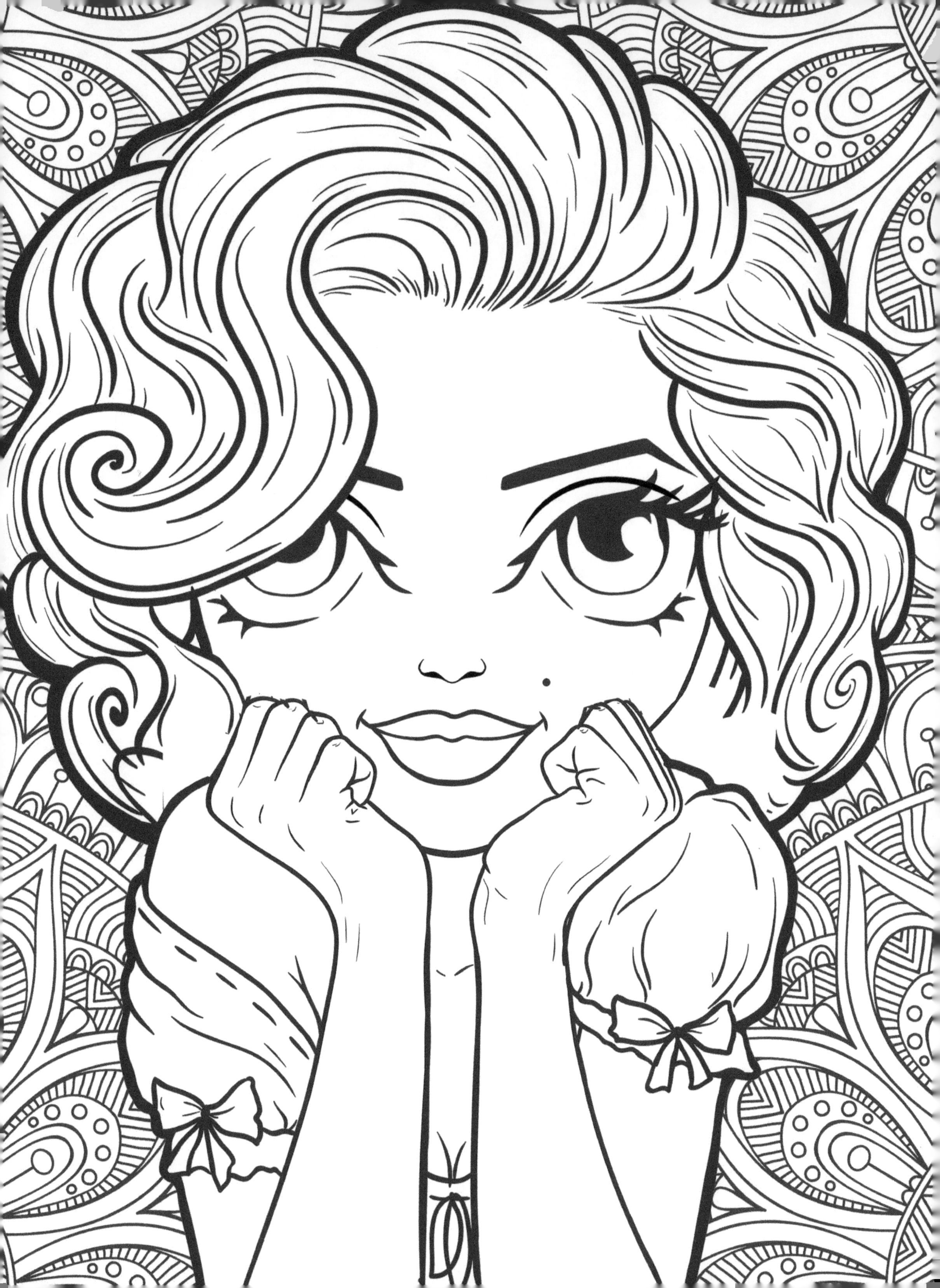

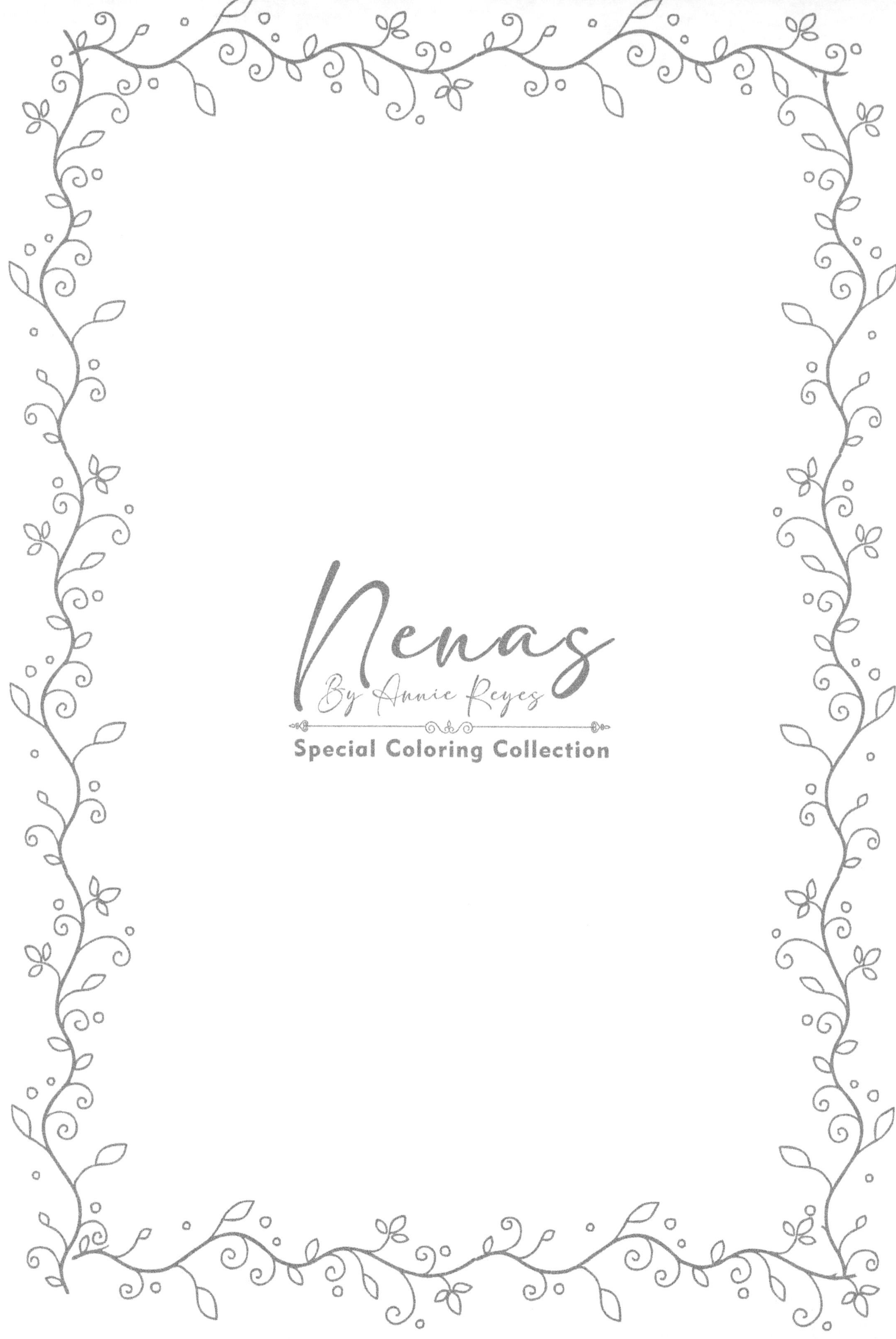
Nenas
By Annie Reyes
Special Coloring Collection

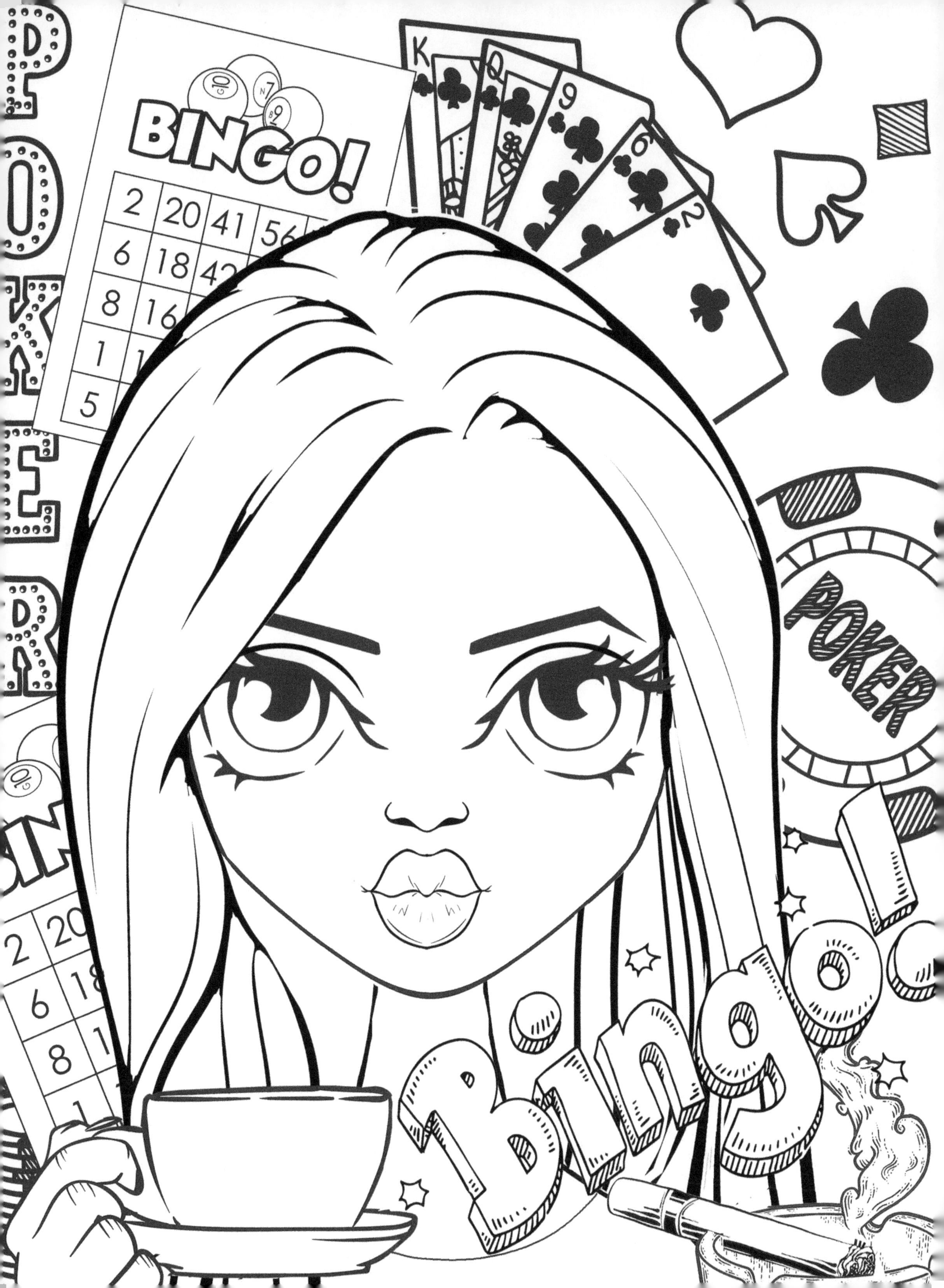

POKER
BINGO!
2 20 41 56
6 18 42
8 16
1 1
5
K
Q
9
2
POKER
bingo
2 20
6 18
8

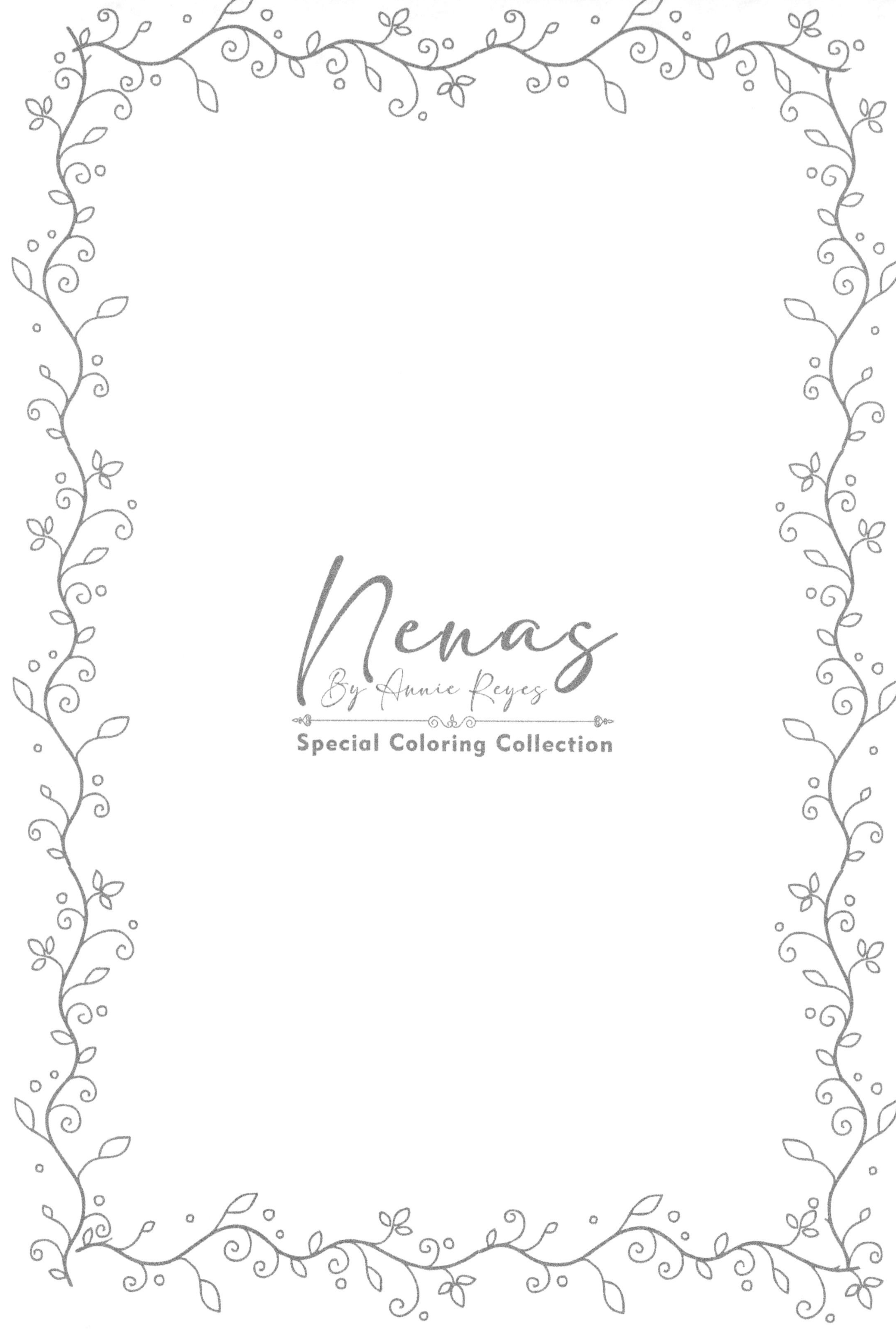

Nenas
By Annie Reyes
Special Coloring Collection

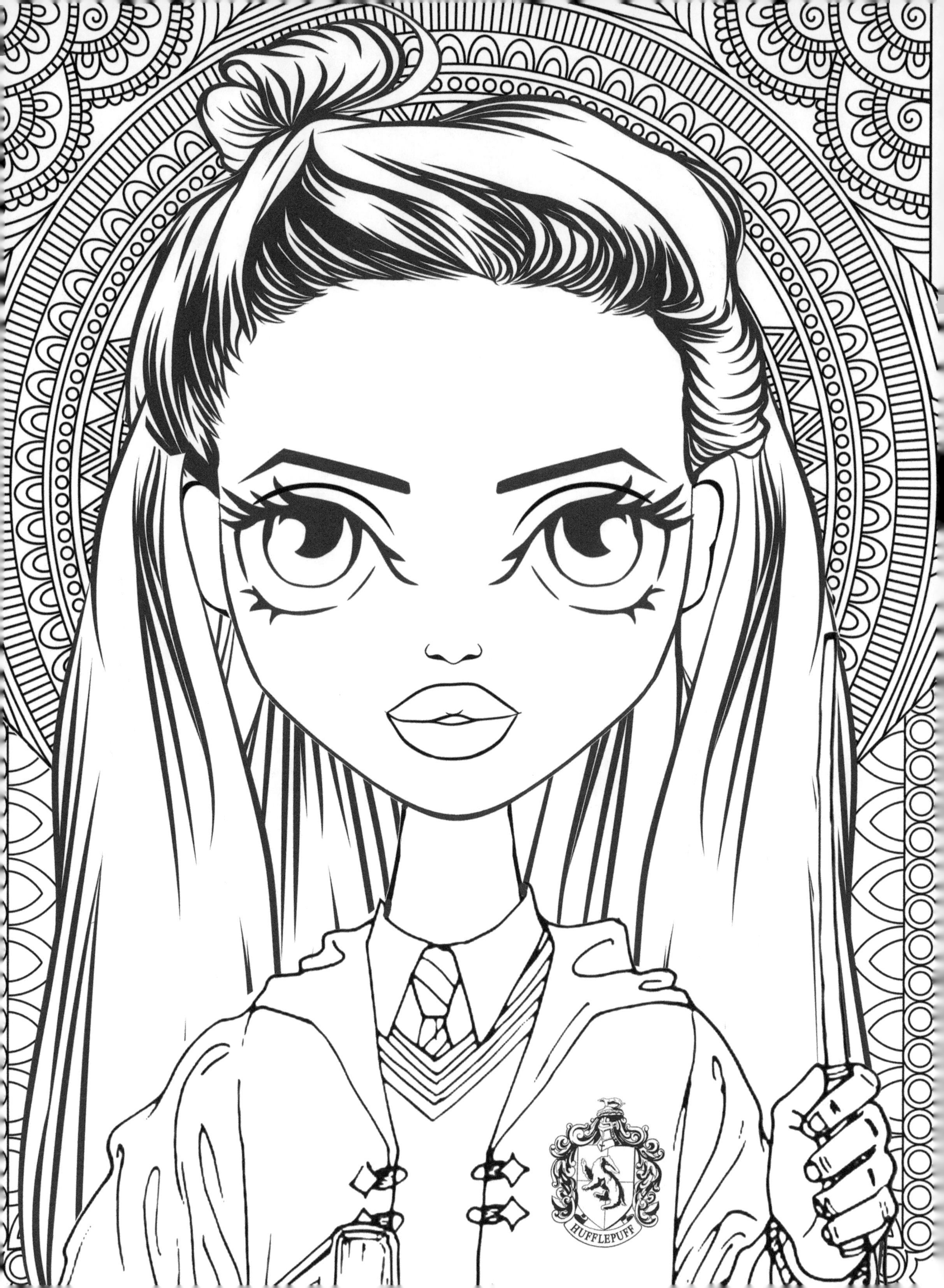

HUFFLEPUFF

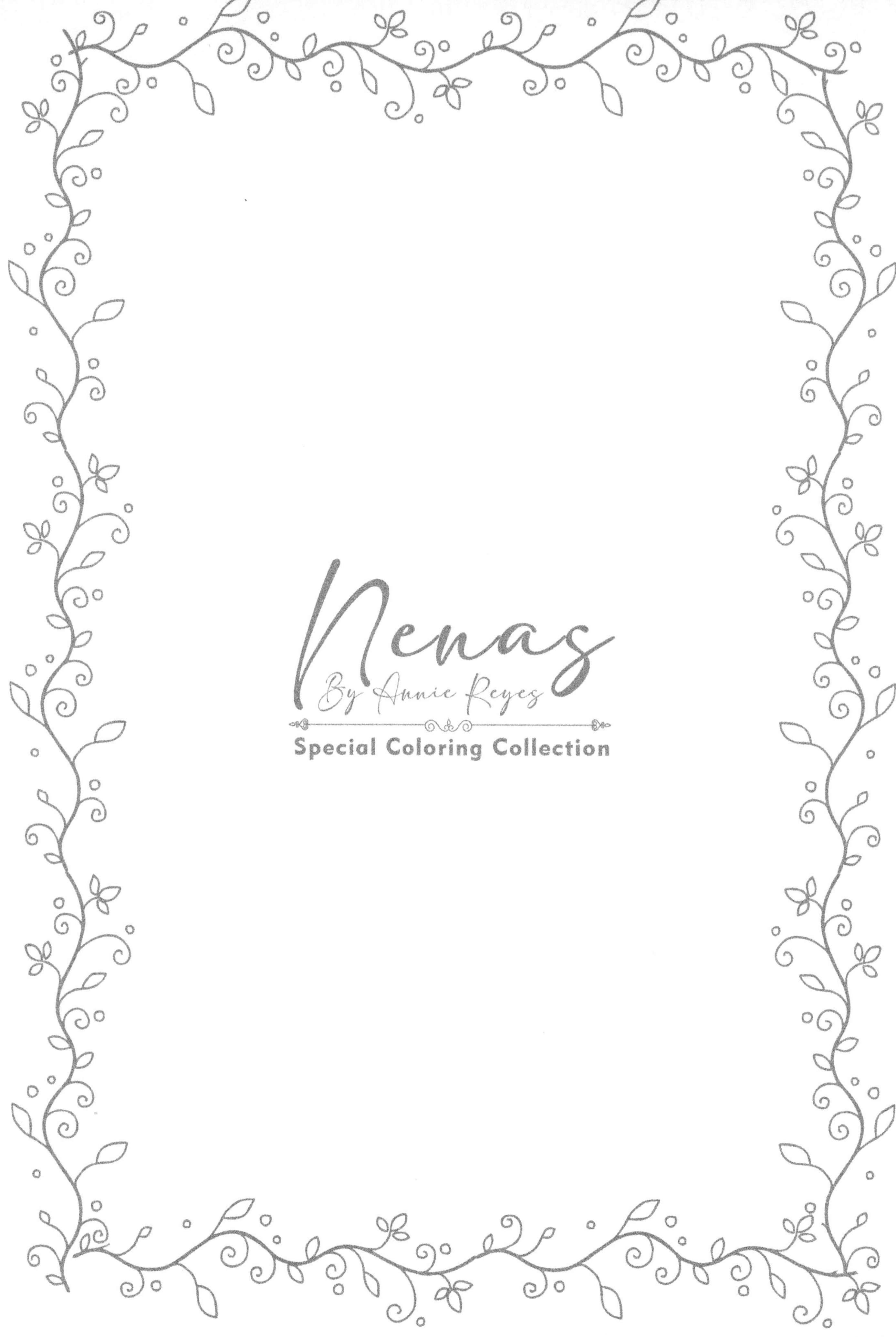

Nenas
By Annie Reyes
Special Coloring Collection

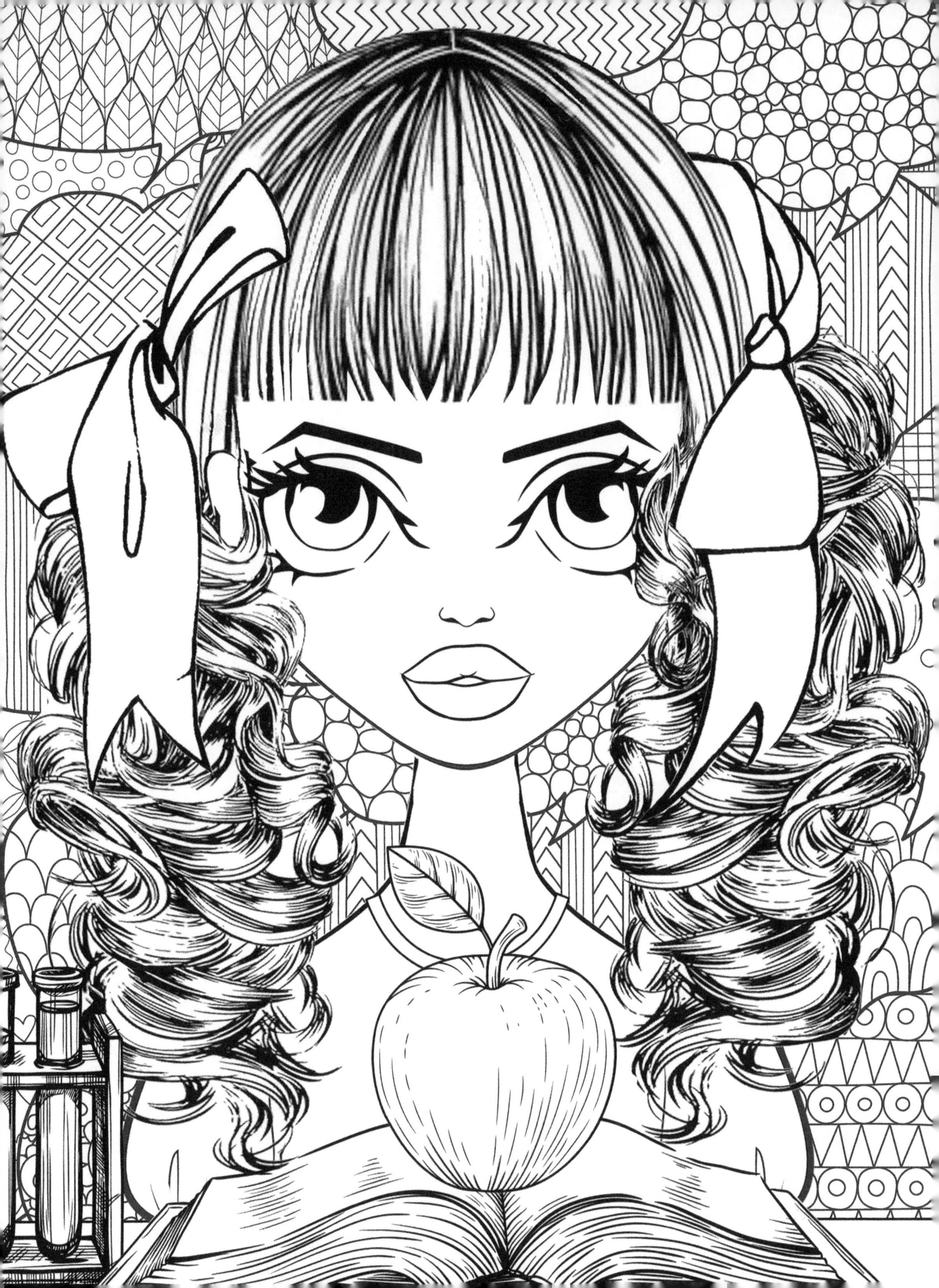

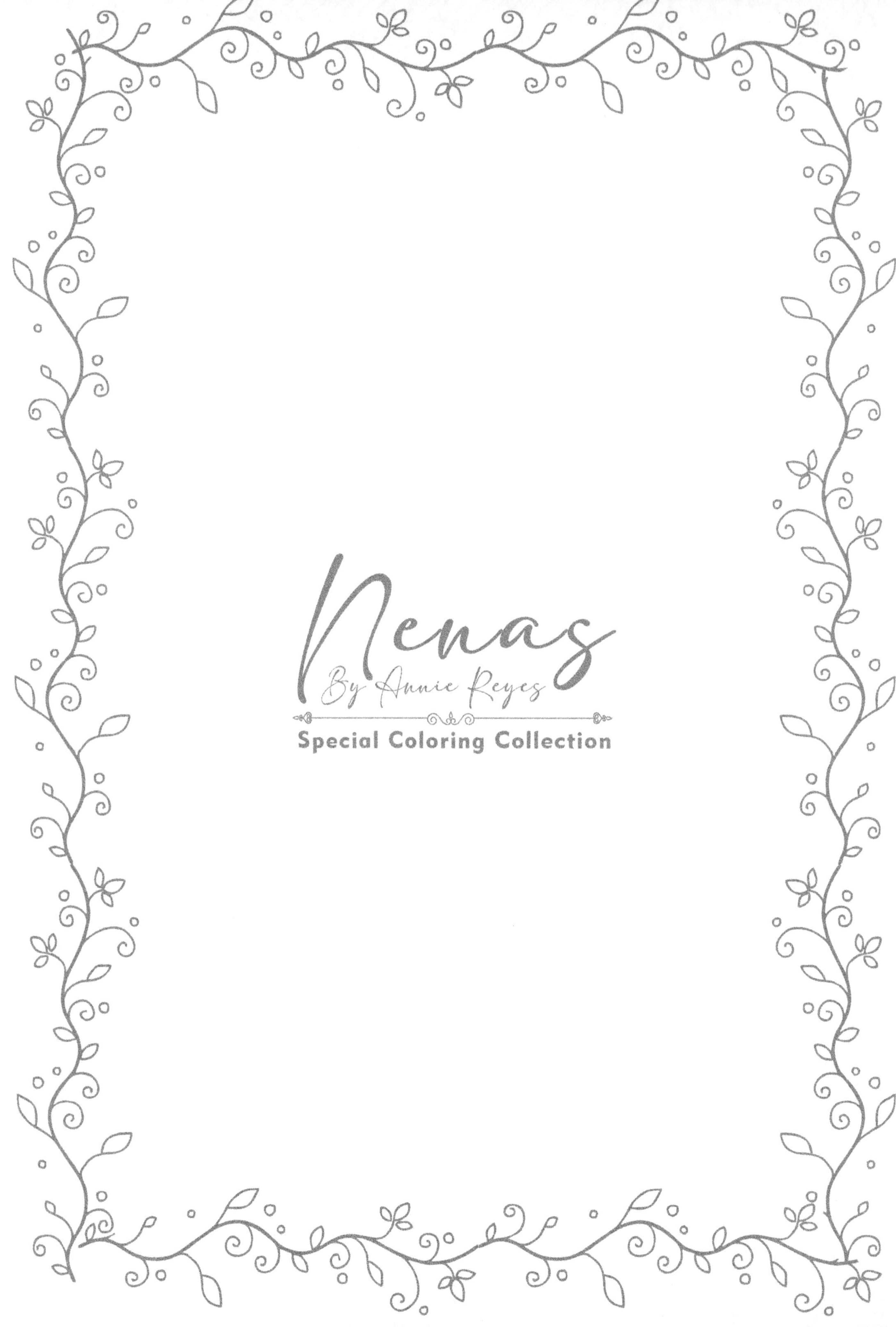

Nenas
By Annie Reyes
Special Coloring Collection

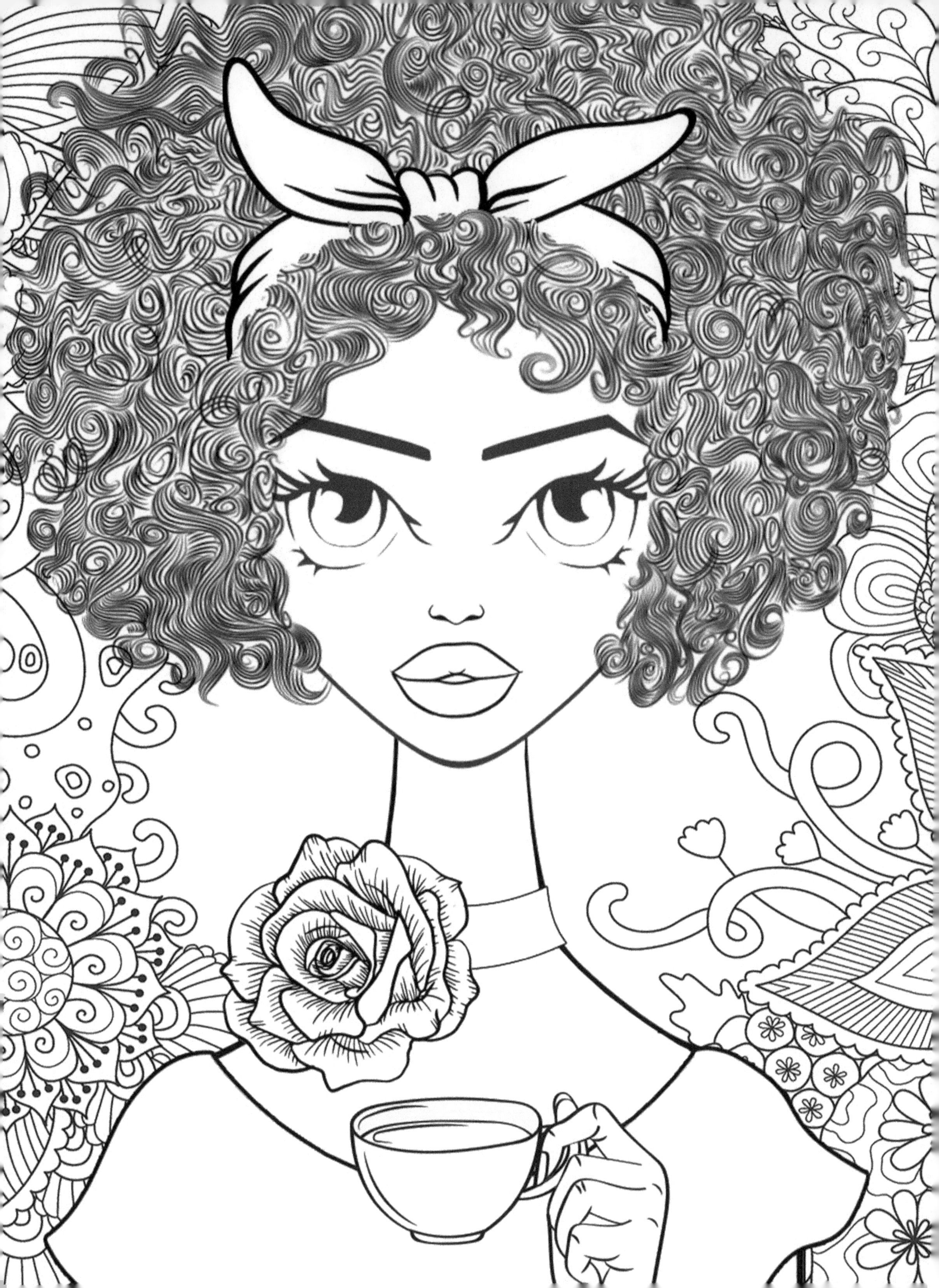

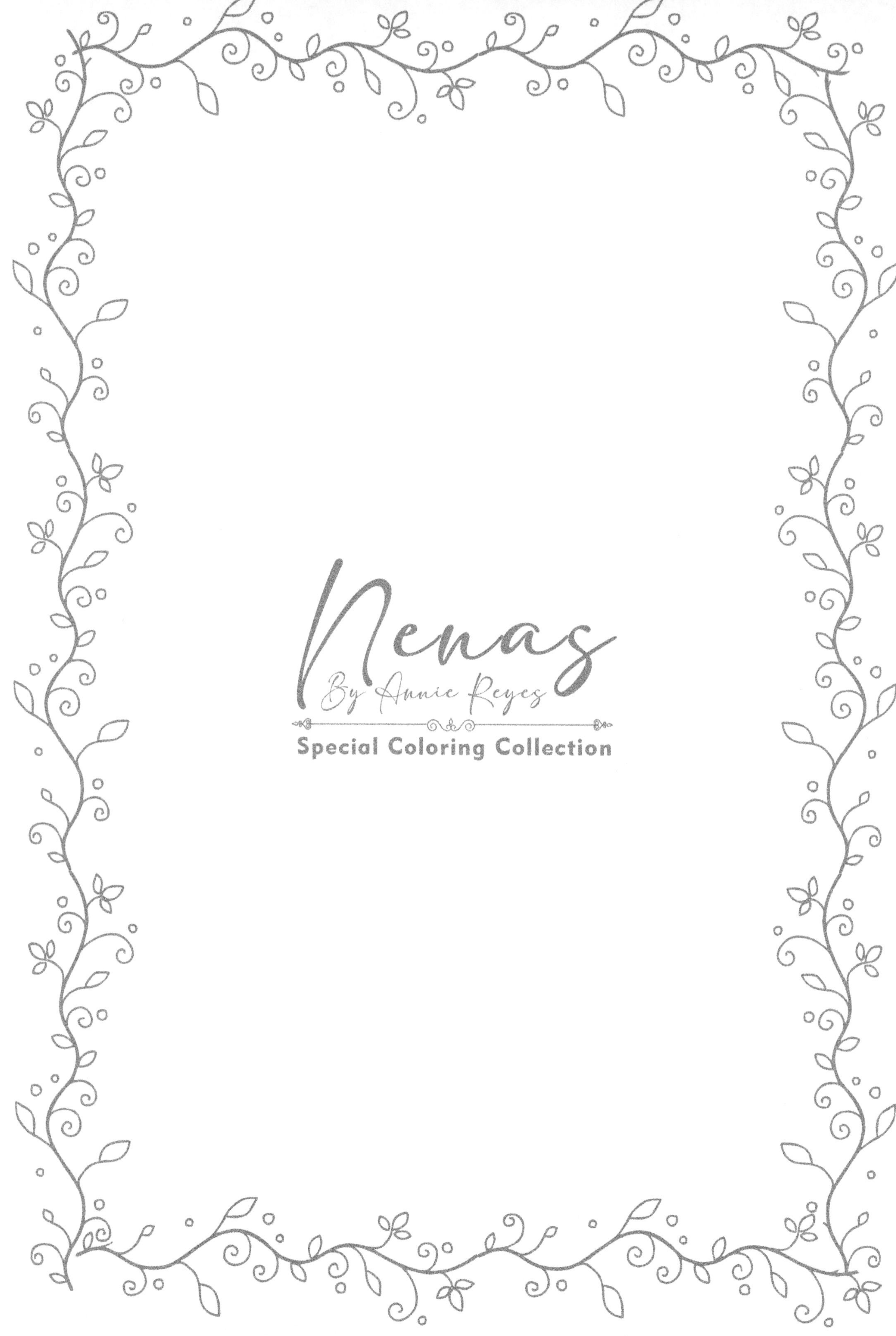

Nenas
By Annie Reyes
Special Coloring Collection

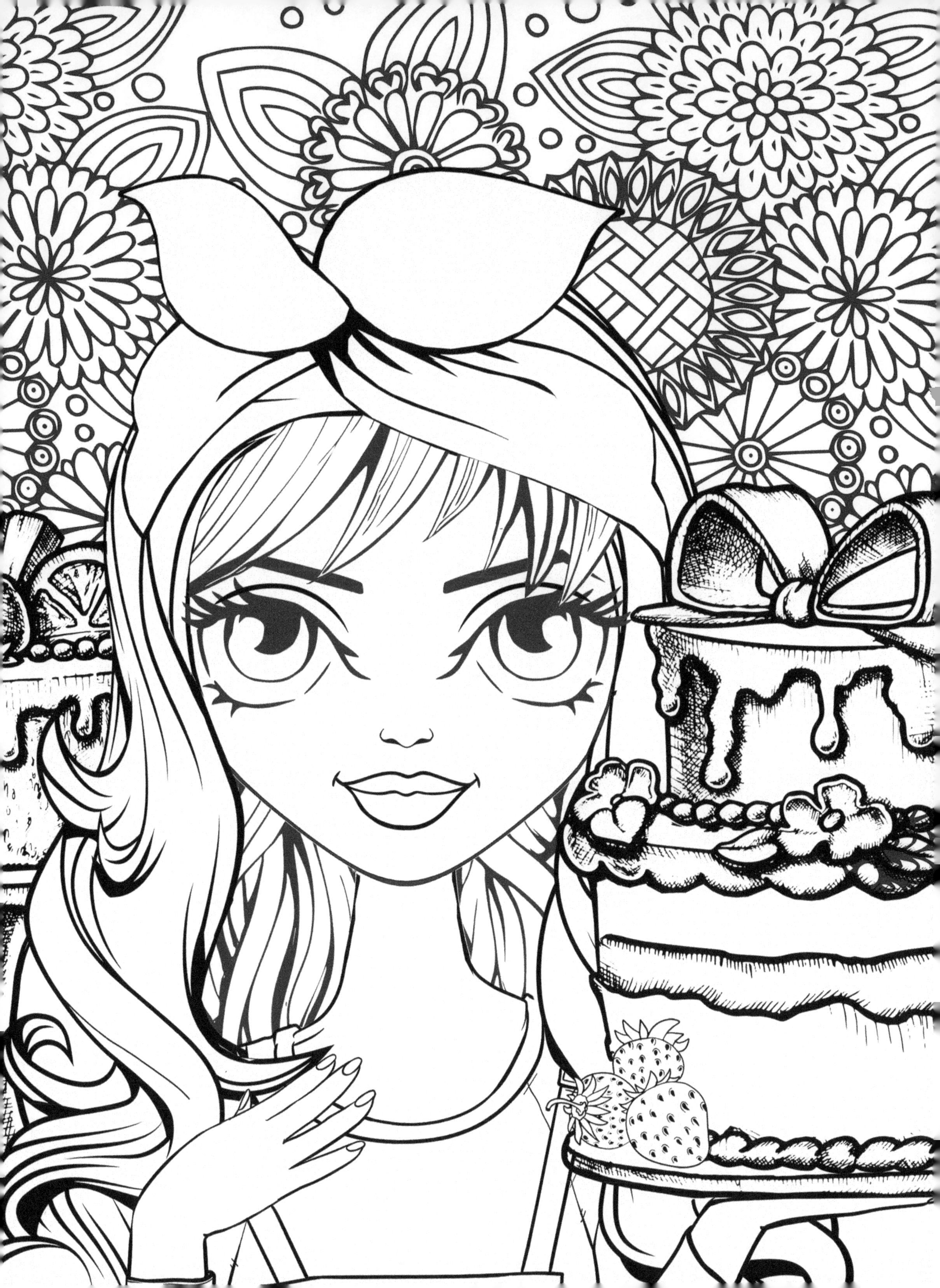

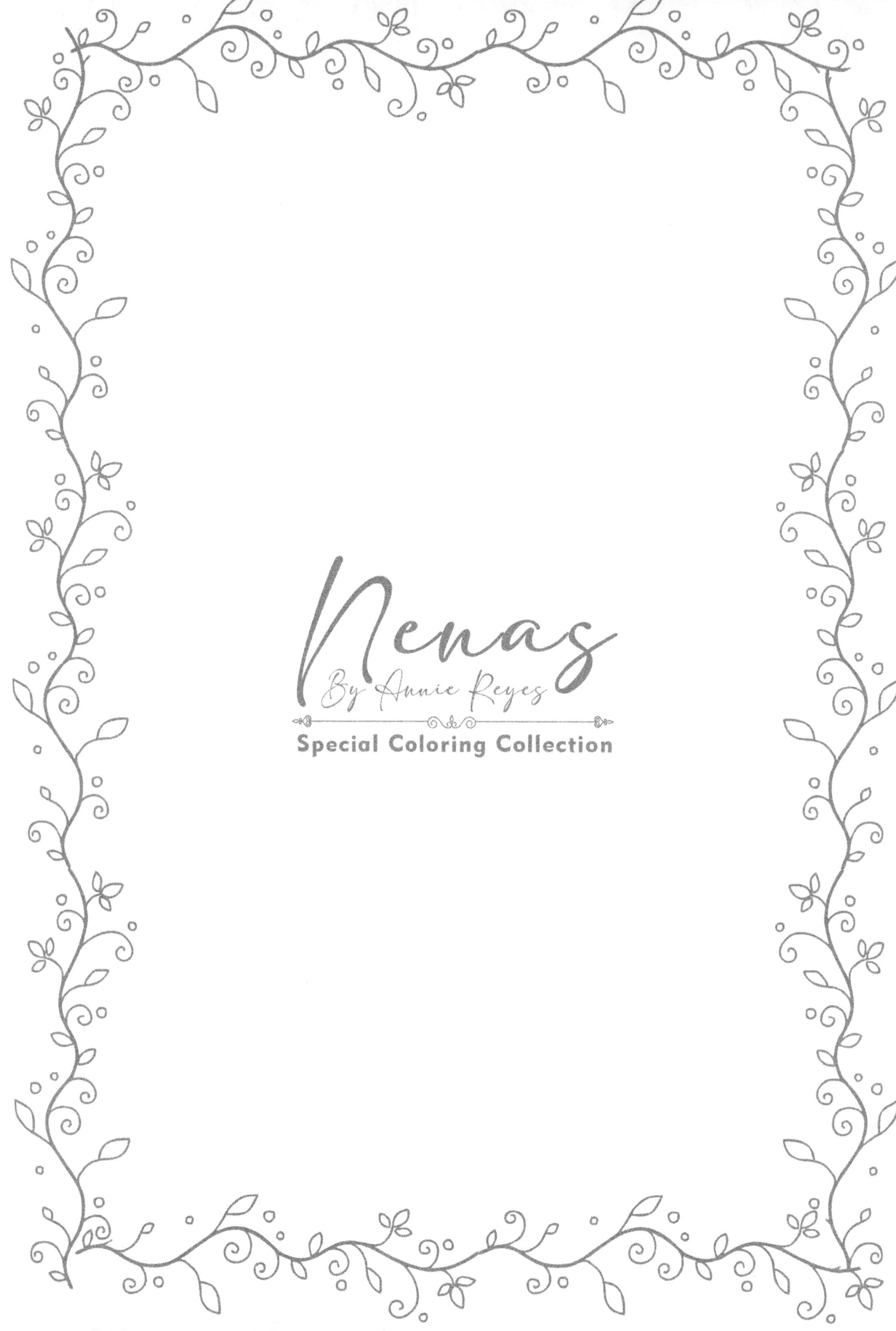
Nenas
By Annie Reyes
Special Coloring Collection

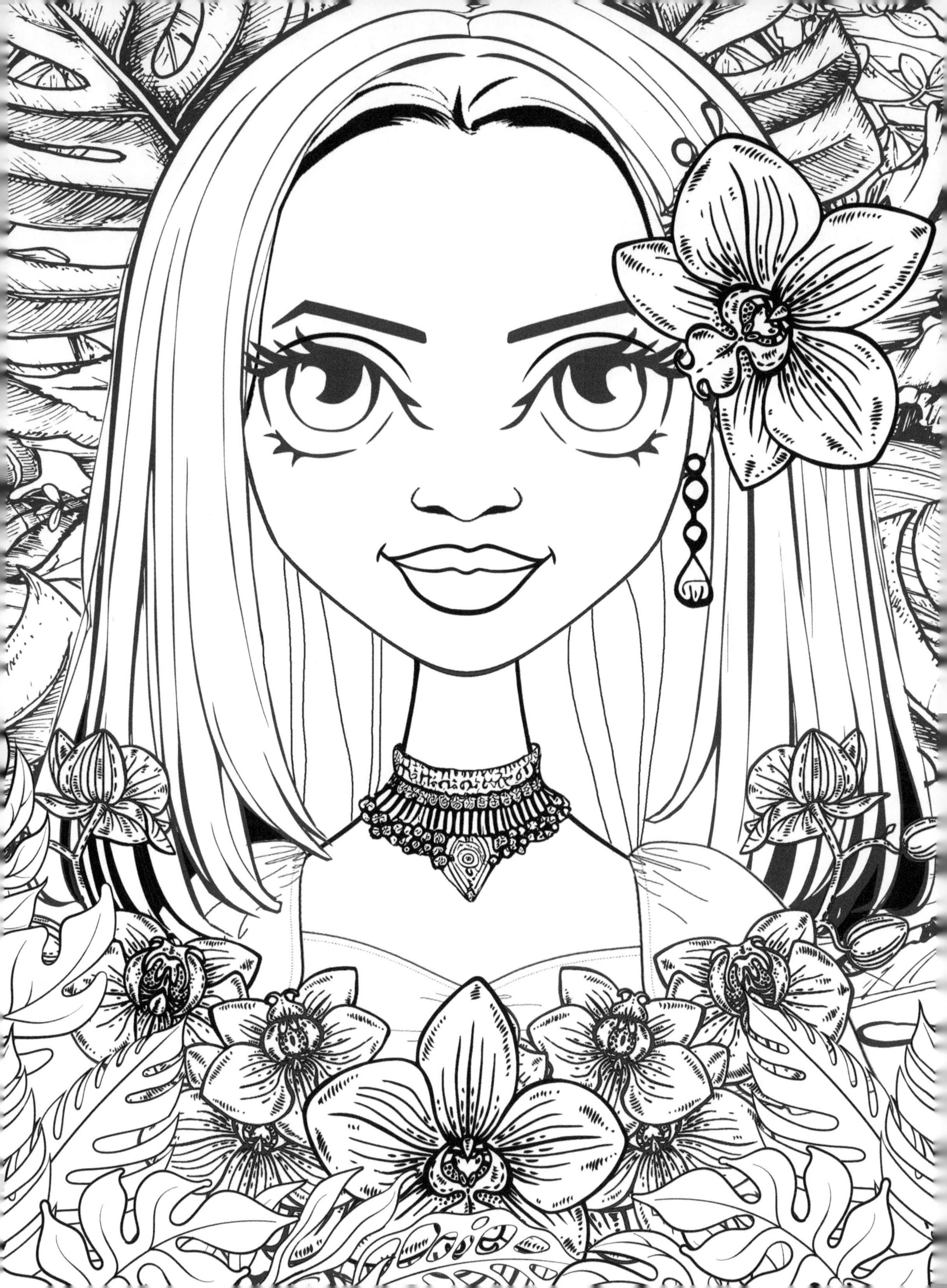

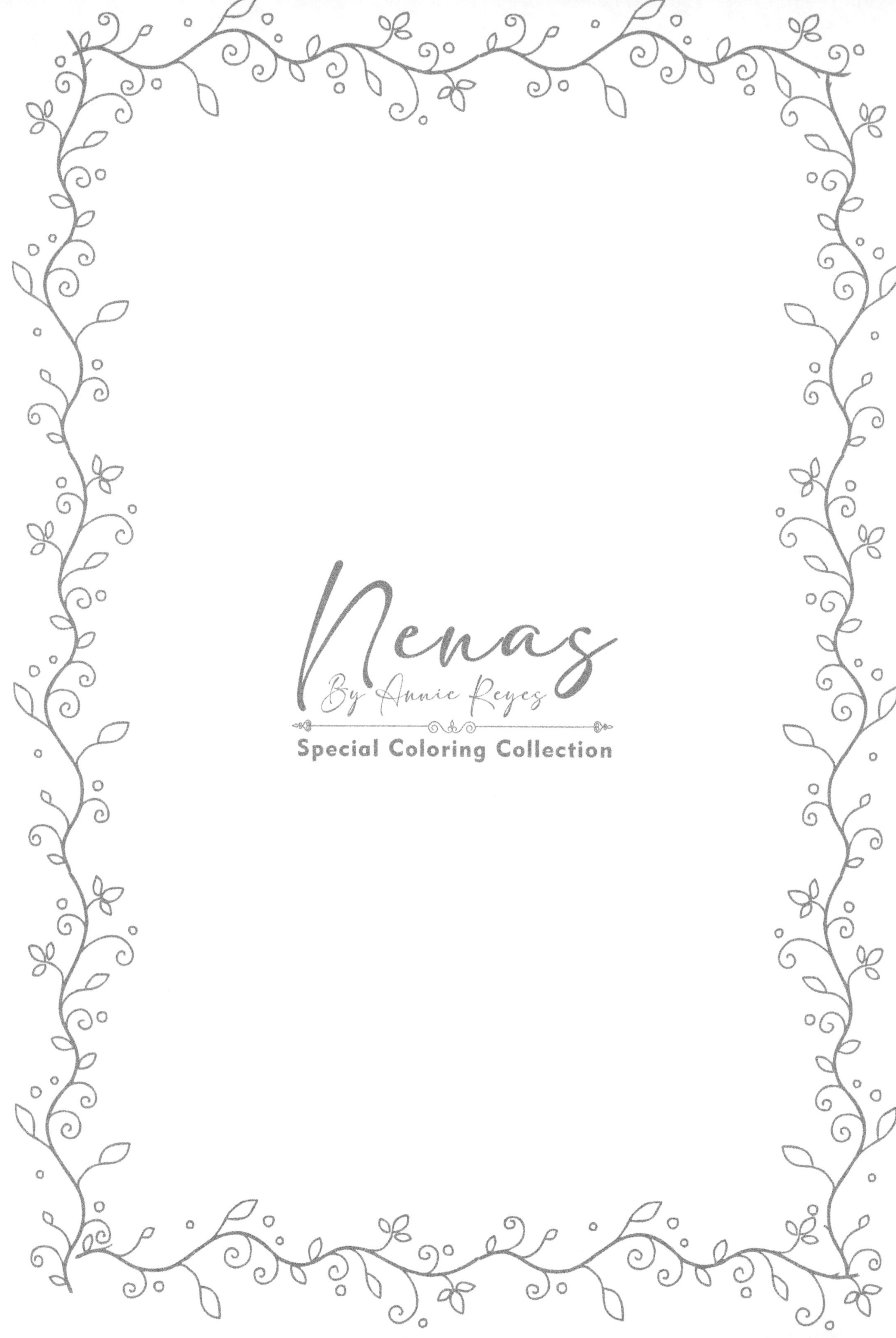

Nenas
By Annie Reyes
Special Coloring Collection

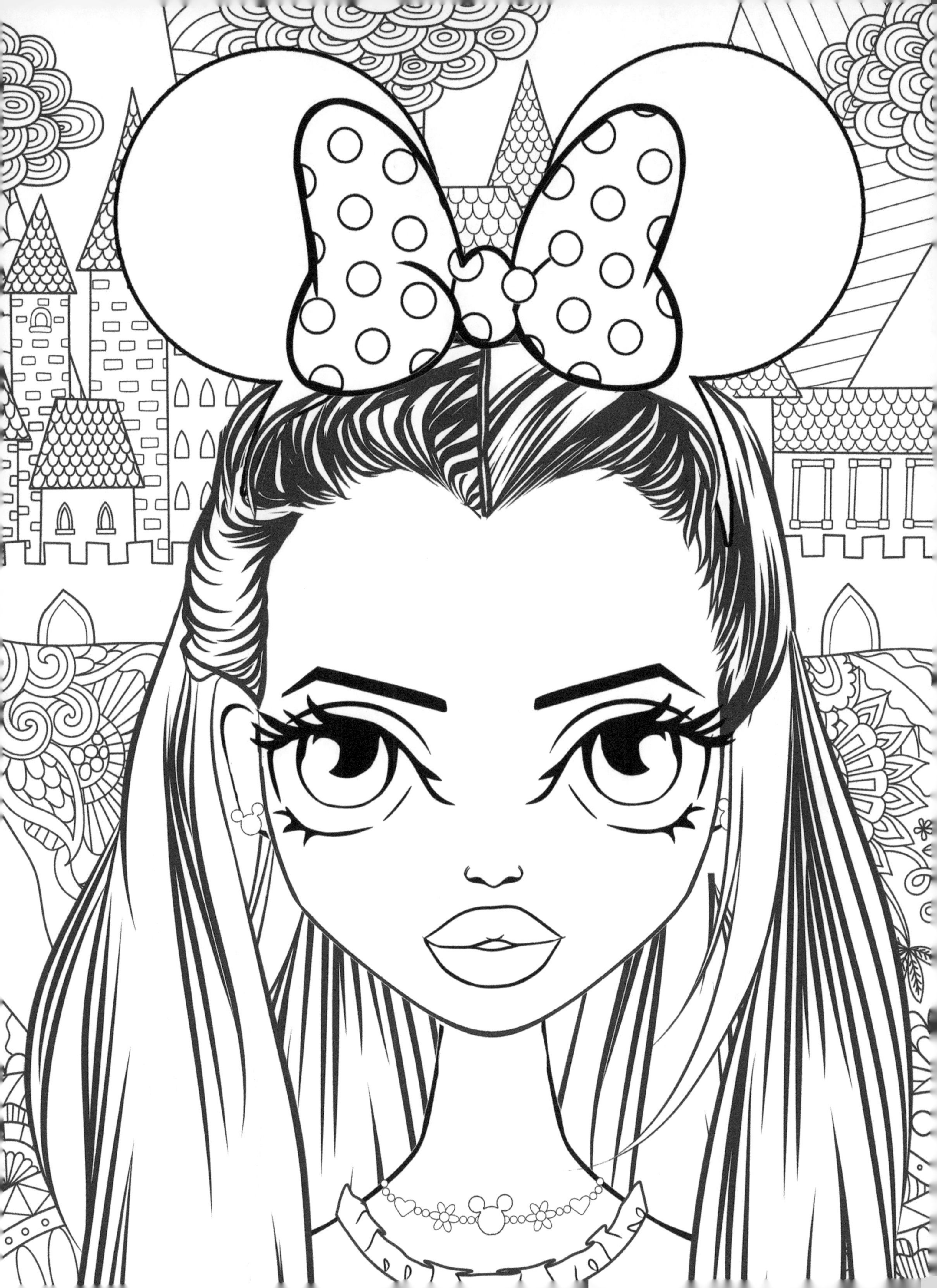

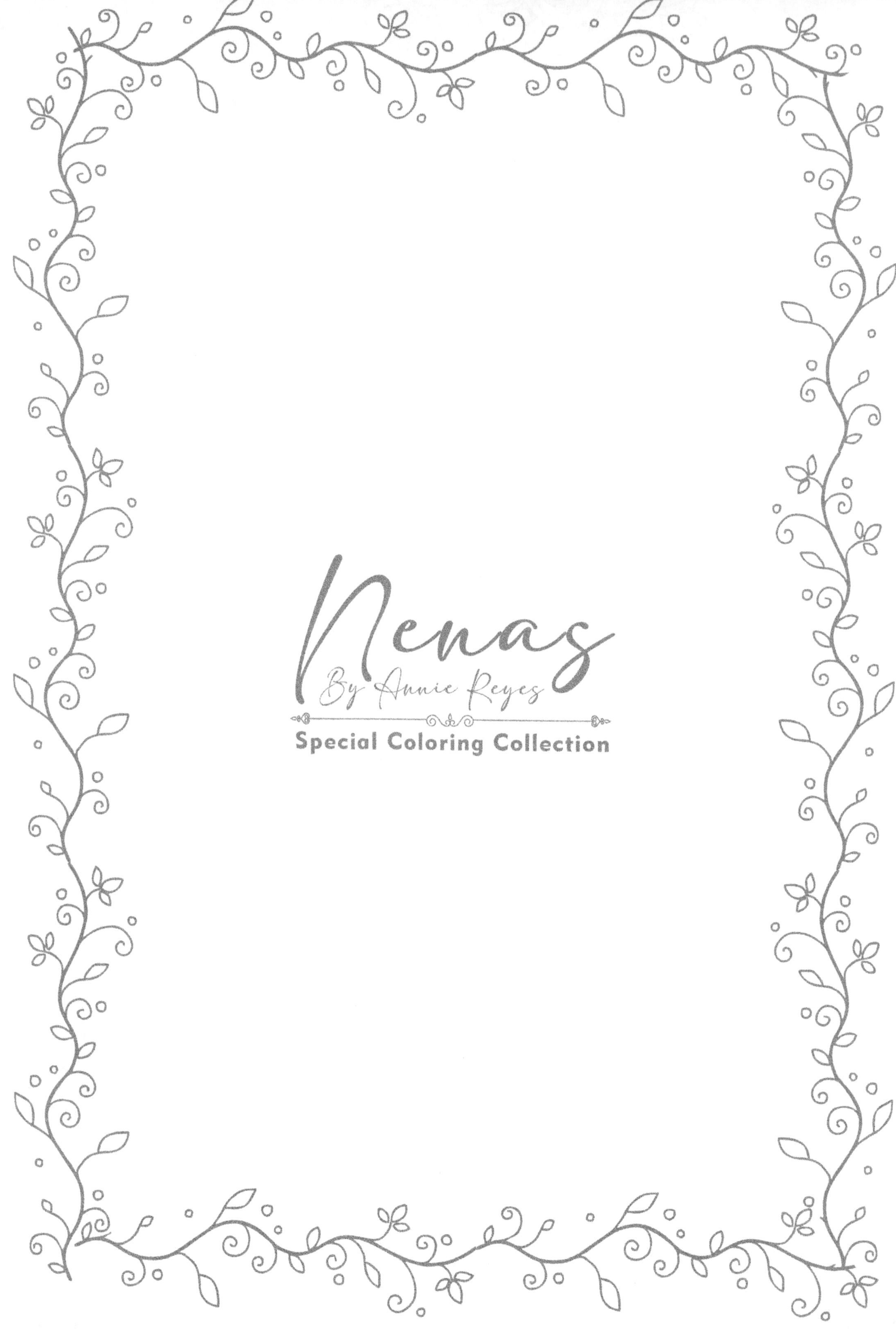

Nenas
By Annie Reyes
Special Coloring Collection

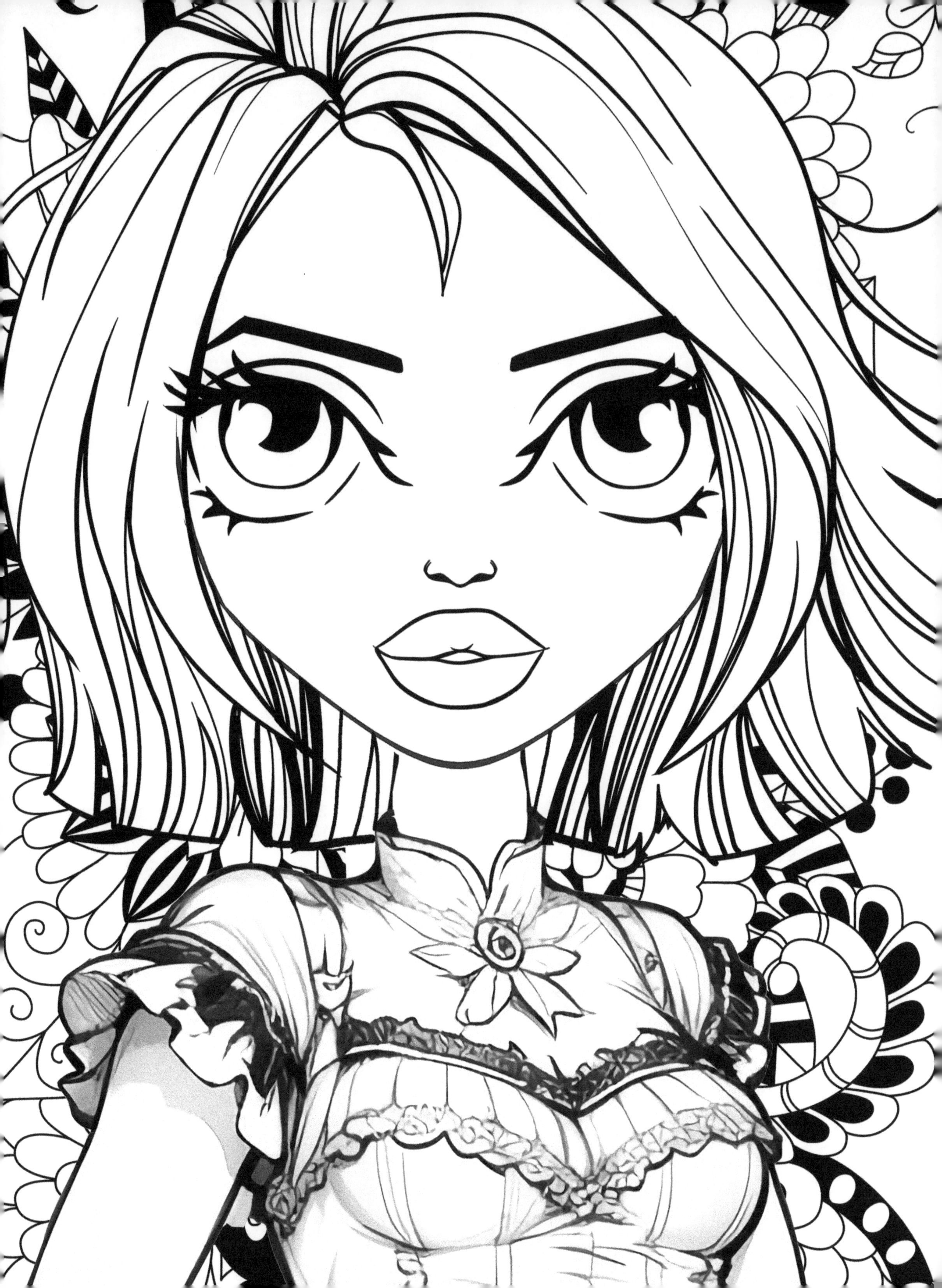

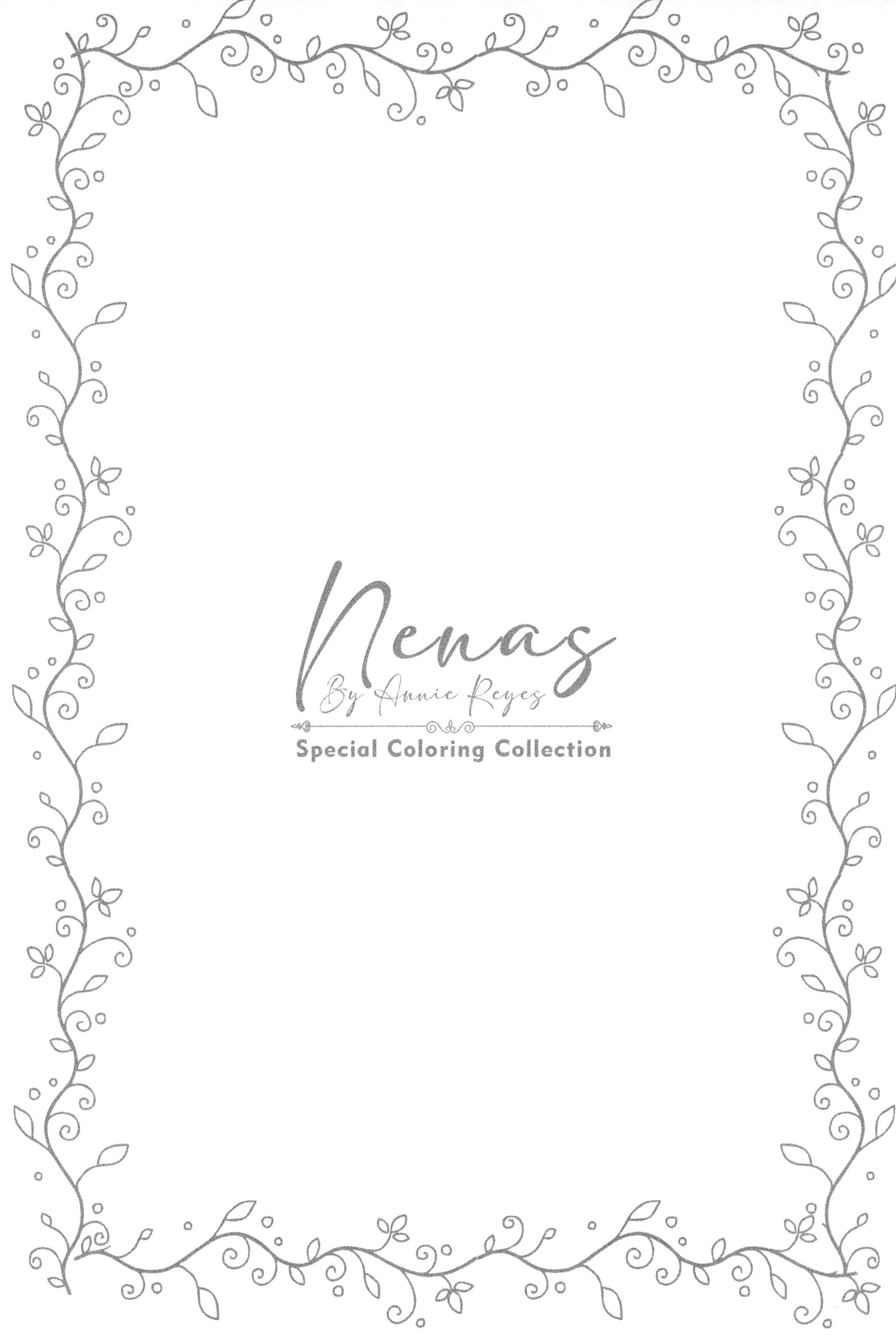

Nenas
By Annie Reyes
Special Coloring Collection

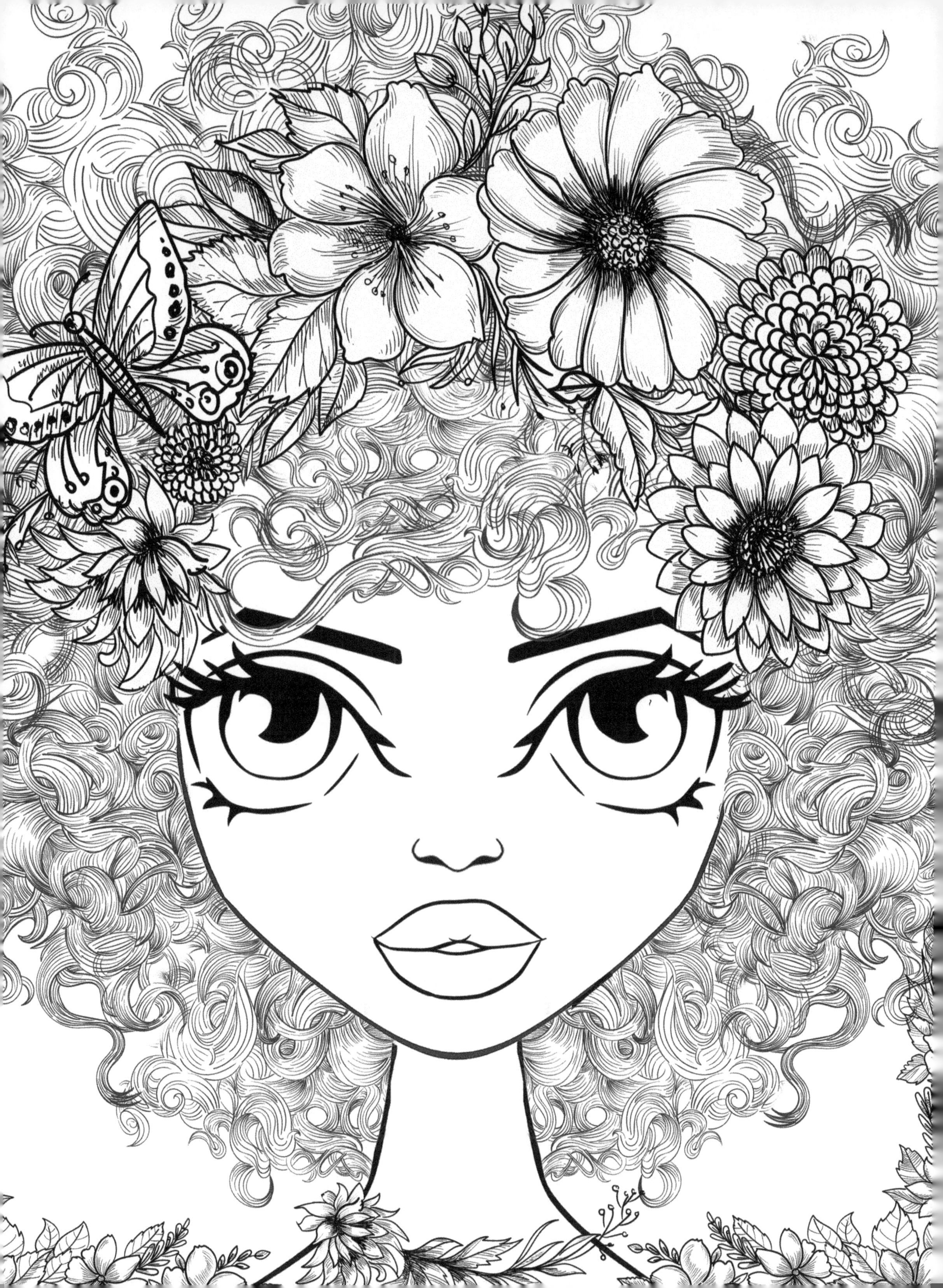

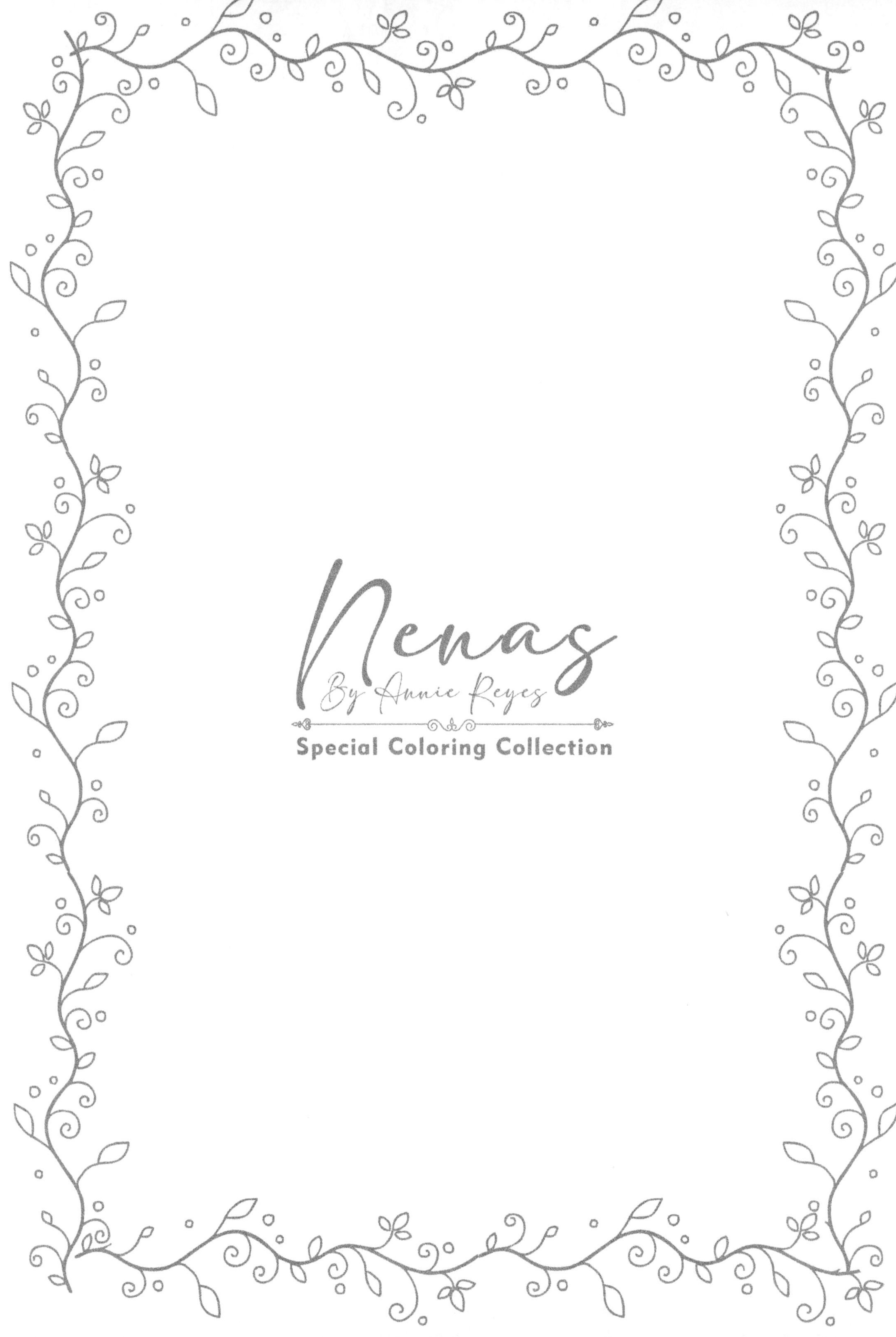
Nenas
By Annie Reyes
Special Coloring Collection